Praise for *The Viking Manifesto*

"Note to self: Read th̶ ̶ ̶ ̶es, then gave us the Nol ̶ ̶ *ing Manifesto* explains ho̶ ̶ er cent of the world's po̶ ̶ ̶ cent of the world's exports.

"Highly recommended. *The Viking Manifesto* makes for an interesting read and may prove a source of inspiration. Its advice is not so much practical and detailed – it is more about getting the spirit of entrepreneurship right and growing your brand in line with the Scandinavian way." **Start Your Business**

"A very readable tour through a culture and approach that rarely gets the attention it deserves. A closer study of the Viking experience can provide useful insights to past triumphs, as well as future trends." **Professional Manager**

To Emeric

from Jo

17/2 2010

The VIKING MANIFESTO

The VIKING MANIFESTO

The Scandinavian approach to business and blasphemy

Steve Strid and Claes Andréasson

Marshall Cavendish
Business

Hardback edition first published in 2007

This paperback edition published in 2008 by

Marshall Cavendish Limited
Fifth Floor
32–38 Saffron Hill
London EC1N 8FH
T: +44 (0)20 7421 8120
F: +44 (0)20 7421 8121
sales@marshallcavendish.co.uk
www.marshallcavendish.co.uk

A CIP record for this book is available from the British Library

ISBN 978-0-462-09932-3

Printed and bound in Great Britain by
CPI Bookmarque, Croydon, CRO 4TD

Beware, the half-wise are everywhere

from "Hávamál", a 13th-century Viking poem

A note from our lawyer to yours

All assault, rape, drug use, theft, property damage and killing of monks referred to in this book are meant for literary and metaphorical* purposes only.

These activities are immoral and/or illegal in most countries and should not be tried at home.

* **metaphor** – a figure of speech where one concept is compared to another for purposes of description; a comparison used for symbolic purposes and not meant to represent a real thing.

The latest in globalization from AD 900

The Vikings were heathens; they didn't play by the rules. When they invaded, it wasn't with huge armies; it was with a better idea. That idea was simple: surprise attacks and brutal plundering. The Vikings carefully picked a target and struck without warning, armed to the teeth and high on mead and mushrooms. They were strong believers in globalization and bloodshed.

Yet, these same barbarians knew the world was round 500 years before Columbus and built the world's fastest ships. For centuries, they were Europe's most intrepid businessmen, establishing trade routes from Scandinavia to Russia, the Middle East and Africa. They had the world's first working parliament (AD 930) and were the first Europeans to discover North America. They had an egalitarian society in which women enjoyed a measure of equality unheard of until modern times.

Today, the Vikings have built some of the most peaceful and wealthy societies in the world. With a population barely big enough to fill a major city, modern Vikings have created some of the most famous marketing successes in the world. Companies such as IKEA, Lego, Absolut, Volvo, Hennes &

Mauritz, Ericsson, Electrolux, SAAB, ABB, Skanska, SCA and Astra Zeneca have made marketing history, while cultural icons such as the Nobel Prize have become household names. Sweden is even the world's third largest exporter of pop music after the USA and the UK.

The Vikings have become social democrats and models of liberal societies, yet, they still don't play by the rules. The Viking is more soft spoken, but alive and well. Without any army to speak of, they still invade with a better idea and a new approach to marketing, advertising, culture and corporate culture. All very different enterprises with very different things to sell. All with a common denominator.

That common denominator is the Viking Manifesto, an unwritten, yet deeply rooted Scandinavian philosophy. The Viking Manifesto is a new way of building brands, companies and movements, based on ingenuity, teamwork, storytelling, courage and a sense of humour. The Viking Manifesto describes a new way of doing business based on common sense, common decency and surprise attacks. Just as easily called half a dozen other names, the Viking Manifesto is followed by just as many non-Scandinavians and applies to just as many non-profit organizations as private corporations. It's about harnessing the incredible power of cultural clashes in a positive way. Many of these methods are unconventional ideas, bordering on blasphemous. They're new, they're old and they work.

The Vikings are back, and this time they mean business.

The Viking Brand
What's in it for you?

The Vikings left no monuments, no structures, no temples, no churches, no cities, no nation or ethnic group, no cuisine and only a handful of texts. There is little proof they ever existed. Yet somehow, the concept of "the Vikings" is as well known as that of the Romans and the Greeks. In Asia, it is just as likely that the average person on the street will recognize a drawing of a Viking longboat as a drawing of the Coliseum.

Fifty years ago, this could be called by a dozen different names. Today, we call it branding. The Vikings, when they kicked off their boots after a hard day of senseless violence, were motivators, marketers and story-tellers.

And they still are. With a population of just under 20 million for Sweden, Denmark, Norway and Iceland, today's Vikings only account for 0.3 per cent of the world's population, yet produce a whopping 3 per cent of all world exports. Scandinavian products are first-rate, but it is their brands that have swept the world.

So, do they have a secret?

Of course. Modern Vikings have a different mindset, a mindset that makes all the difference. And that's what this book is all about – a different approach to making a name for your company, your product, organization or cause. These methods are as applicable to the corporate world as they are to charities, organizations and anti-globalists. The method explains why advertising doesn't work and why this is good, why competition is nonsense, why reward and punishment are an inferior form of motivation and why money doesn't make the world go round.

As if this isn't blasphemous enough, the Viking Manifesto describes how to create effective PR that no one sees, and explains why lawyers should wait outside.

This book is firmly anchored in Viking culture, yet is not a history book. It uses Scandinavian examples as a philosophical point of departure, yet is not a book about successful Scandinavian companies.

It is a book about doing business with sharp weapons, a sharp wit and a clear conscious.

It's method without the madness.

Map of the book

This book is divided into two sections: *Marketing* and *Corporate Culture*. Each section focuses on the principles and attitudes that make up the Viking Manifesto.

Feel free to replace the word *Marketing* with *Promotion*, *Starting a Movement*, *Making a Go of It* or anything else that is more applicable to your area of endeavour (charity, activism, education, etc.). The same goes for *Corporate Culture*. *Organizational Culture*, *Motivation*, *Leadership*, *Community* or *Management* will also do just fine.

Contents

Manifesto: a written statement declaring publicly the intentions, principles, motives or views of its issuer.

Introduction   1

    "No one will ever buy a Swedish Vodka!"   1

    Let the blasphemy begin   4

PART I: MARKETING

PRINCIPLES

  1 If there's something you'd rather be doing, do it   11

  2 Invade with a good idea   13

  3 Visionaries often look back   14

  4 A change of course, but never a change of heart   16

  5 A few words before we set sail: learn the basics   19

  6 Plan your attack   31

  7 Use your weaknesses to your advantage   32

  8 Decide which small god to pick on   34

  9 Think small and see the big picture   38

10 Think big and see the small opening   41

11 Even in a war of words, actions speak louder   44

12 Make money on suffering, despair and poverty   47

13 Make money on human decency   49

14 Be humble and rude (rather than arrogant and polite)   51

15 Adopt a target group – people you like or people like you 54

16   Make money by giving things away   57

17   Start innovative, stick to your principles, change   59

18   Blend in by standing out   63

19   Learn the new maths   66

20   Perfect the product   70

21   If your product is really terrible ...   72

22   There are millions of products, but only two brands – be both of them   74

23   Competition is a secondary consideration   78

24   The tools remain the same   81

25   Advertising doesn't work and why this is good   82

26   A good story is worth millions more than it used to be   84

27   Viking Zen (or summer fashion at 30 below zero)   87

28   Go against type   90

29   Use education as marketing   93

PART II: CORPORATE CULTURE

PRINCIPLES

30   Pillaging, plundering and other family values   99

31   Everyone's in charge   101

32   Learn to make the right mistakes   104

33   Problems are a manager's best friend   107

34   Put berserkers in the front of the boat (... but don't let them steer)   110

35   Put violence in perspective and take it out of your business   114

36   Make a note: slavery is an administrative nightmare   116

37   Empower your women   120

38   Competition is nonsense   124

39   If you want to motivate, forget reward and punishment   127

40 Talk is cheap, but still overpriced   130
41 Resurrect the lost art of decision-making   132
42 Keep people honest   134
43 Plagiarize the plagiarist – an original idea worth copying   136
44 Put lawyers in the last boat   139
45 Use creative accounting for a better world   142
46 Controversy is great, if you're right   145
47 Rethink money   146
48 Two approaches to dealing with crisis – proactive or poodle   150
49 Take marketing studies with a pinch of salt   153
50 Don't leave luck to chance   155

    Appendix: The latest thing from AD 900   161
    Bibliography   163
    About the authors   167
    Illustration credits   168

The VIKING MANIFESTO

Introduction

"No one will ever buy a Swedish vodka!"

The project was doomed to failure.

In 1978, half a dozen leading marketing consultants from the US and Europe had spoken. They backed up their conclusions with feasibility studies, marketing analyses, consumer surveys and the iron-clad common sense that comes with top-dollar credentials. They had spent hundreds of hours on both sides of the Atlantic staring at vodka shelves and they were adamant.

"No one will ever buy a Swedish vodka. Forget this whole Absolut thing."

V&S Vin och Sprit AB (The Swedish Wine & Spirits Group) listened. After all, they were a state-owned monopoly in a country most people couldn't find on a map. They had had a national monopoly on the production and importation of all wine and spirits since 1917 and the little export experience they could look back upon had been a quiet disaster.

Some months after the consultants had rendered their verdict, President Lars Lindmark and Chairman of the Board Egon Jacobsson approached the board of directors for a green light for exporting Absolut. They were given a minuscule budget and a pat on the back. When they said that Absolut could in the near future make up half of the company's sales, they got more than a few laughs.

It was hard to see that the company had much of a future as a player on the international spirits market; a market dominated by conglomerates, gangsters and multinationals that were a little of both. The project didn't have a chance. What they did have was a vodka called *Absolut rent brännvin* – literally translated, "Absolutely pure vodka".

In 1879, a hundred years earlier, "Absolutely pure vodka" had taken the Swedish market by storm. At its height at the end of the nineteenth century, exports of the vodka totalled over 100 million litres a year. In 1979, the brand would celebrate a century on the Swedish domestic market.

The project went on. The bottle was redesigned. The new bottle would have a modern look, yet would celebrate the 500-year vodka-making tradition that had produced it. After many false starts, the team decided on a design based on an eighteenth-century Swedish apothecary bottle. A marketing concept was outlined: the bottle and a quality statement; no people, no lifestyle and a little wit. "Made in Sweden" would stay in the background.

V&S Vin och Sprit set its sights on the US market and went looking for a distributor and a US ad agency. They were a long-shot: the major distributors turned them down. They had little money: the major ad agencies turned them down.

Finally, Carillon, a small importer in New Jersey, took the product into its assortment, which consisted of Grand Marnier and a few other niche products. The company had 60 employees and was headed by an eccentric Frenchman, Michel Roux, who saw a future for the Swedish vodka.

At about the same time, the newly started New York office of the European agency TBWA took on the task of turning the Stockholm brief into a selling campaign. They were still trying to establish themselves and saw the account as a creative challenge. David Wachsman and Associates were brought in as a PR agency to generate editorial media coverage that would make the limited ad budget go further.

Over the next two decades, Absolut went on to make both marketing and PR history. From an obscure local vodka to the world's third best-selling spirits brand in two decades, Absolut is one of the great branding successes of all times. And it was done breaking many of the most basic branding rules:

- *Have a large marketing budget*. Absolut didn't.
- *Think big, advertise to a mass market*. Absolut used only limited print ads in specialized magazines.

- *Make sure the product screams from the shelf*. Absolut had a clear bottle without a paper label.
- *Watch every move the competitors make*. Absolut basically ignored the competition.
- *Use people and lifestyle*. Absolut had nothing but its bottle.
- *Take it for granted that people are idiots*. Absolut spoke with intelligence.

It was obvious that Absolut's marketing was new and different. What was less obvious was that it was part of a larger picture: many Scandinavian companies have been successful in creating strong brands using similar approaches.

A pattern was emerging; a method was begging to be defined.

The Viking Manifesto was waiting to be drafted.

Let the blasphemy begin

The Viking Manifesto is all about flirting with blasphemy: having an original idea and a different way of communicating it.

Viking brands, like the Viking raids of centuries ago, came from nowhere, yet managed to succeed against all odds. Viking brands are trend-setters, yet all have living ties with the past. Most of these brands have brought back a bit of dignity to advertising, marketing and PR. They speak softly, yet make themselves heard. These brands have succeeded on their own terms. And they have two values which have long ago fallen into disfavour in marketing circles: courage and a sense of humour.

When we tried to define what successful ingredients were a common denominator in Scandinavian success stories, we found a number of cultural traits that pointed back in time. Modern Scandinavia is a poster child for modern values: humanitarianism, democracy and free enterprise. A thousand years ago, Vikings were making wine snifters out of the skulls of their enemies. Today, they're selling furniture in flat packages. Vikings quickly learned that some of the qualities that made them successful in pillage and plunder also made them successful merchants. Vikings came to the conclusion that however profitable their pirating was, there was no future in it, especially as after a few hundred years the element of surprise was starting to wear off. They decided that international commerce was the only sensible future. It was a powerful idea that is still controversial if you look at the state of the world.

The simple truth of the matter is that in the long run, mutual gain is more profitable than theft.

No, really.

PART I

MARKETING

The Viking longboat was small, unimpressive and devastating. These boats, measuring between 40 and 100 feet (16–36 metres) long were by far the fastest ships of their day. They were surprisingly seaworthy and could be carried or towed for long distances over land. This meant they could do the apparently impossible – not only could they land anywhere, they could even travel cross-country by hopping from river to river. And what could be a bigger surprise than being attacked by a fleet of boats from inland?

This is what the Viking Manifesto is all about.

PRINCIPLES

· 1 ·

If there's something you'd rather be doing, do it

The coward believes he will live forever
If he holds back in the battle,
But in old age he shall have no peace
Though spears have spared his limbs

– from "Hávamál"

THERE'S ONE THING MOST people take with them when they die – their dreams. Much of the greyness of everyday life comes from the simple fact that so many of us would rather be doing something else. In business, in government, even in charities and the arts.

Life is not a play: it's not even a dress rehearsal. Those who play a part, instead of living a life, miss out on more than they think. Nothing of any significance has ever been achieved without risk.

The Vikings' idea of heaven – Valhalla – was a reward for bravery on earth. In this heaven, you would fight all day and die, but would be healed each night before a grand feast at the

11

table of the gods. The worst thing imaginable for a Viking was dying of old age. This belief, along with a certain amount of substance abuse, made them fearless in battle.

The Viking method of doing business today, just as it was 1200 years ago, is based on a certain amount of risk. In Viking times, risk meant the possibility of getting a sharp object thrust through your skull. Today, the sharpest object you're likely to encounter is a pair of scissors cutting your Visa card in half.

Risk isn't what it used to be. But dreams are as grand as ever.

The first step of the Viking method is deciding what you really want and accepting the risk that comes with it.

· 2 ·

Invade with a good idea

The mind alone knows what is near the heart,
Each is his own judge
– from "Hávamál"

SOMEONE ONCE SAID TO a friend that he had a great idea, but that he was worried someone might steal it. The friend answered that if his idea was the least bit original, he would have to fight to the death to get anyone to take any notice of it whatsoever.

History is full of famous rejections. The Beatles were turned down by a famous manager because he was certain that guitar groups were going out of style. George Orwell's *Animal Farm* was rejected because it was anti-Russian. Steve Jobs's idea for a home computer was rejected by Atari, and so on.

Good ideas have a way of succeeding against all odds. Good ideas have an amazing power over the human psyche. All they need is a little timing and a lot of push.

Do you have a good idea? You should know. Time to do something about it.

· 3 ·

Visionaries often look back

Take notice of the past if you would achieve originality
– Einar Benediktsson (1864–1940), Icelandic poet and lawyer

IN LITERATURE, SCIENCE, the humanities, music and business, innovators are often people who have a strong connection to the past. Visionaries often spend as much time looking back as they do looking forward. Even in the most technological fields, great leaps forward are often inspired by the past. The movement of boats and trains inspired Einstein in his theory of relativity; the two Steves behind Apple were childishly clicking away on naive icons while the rest of the computer world was getting on with the progressive business of typing white backslashes on a blue screen.

People who have lost touch with their past are at a disadvantage when it comes to realizing their future. People with vision look in all directions.

And now for some really bad mushrooms ...

For special occasions (burning down an English monastery, for example) some Vikings took powdered fly agaric, a narcotic mushroom. Fly agaric (Amanita muscaria), has been used as a fly poison and may have been used in the ritual soma drink of the ancient Hindus and in the Zoroastrians' haoma. Fly agaric, unlike the Latin American psychedelic mushrooms (Psilocybe mexicana and Stropharia cubensis), has not been widely studied, but is thought to produce hallucinations and increase strength and endurance.

Closely related mushrooms include death caps (A. phalloides) and destroying angels (A. bispongera, A. ocreata, A. verna, and A. virosa). The first will put you in a respirator with bleeding bowels, the second in a pine box.

Handpicked mushroom omelette, anyone?

◆ 4 ◆

A change of course,
but never a change of heart

*Of the three start-ups I've been involved in, not one has made money
on what they set out to market. Not one would have succeeded if
they had stuck to the original business plan*

– Robert Young, founder of Red Hat

EVERY HISTORICAL OR GEOGRAPHICAL journey is preceded
by a mental one. The Vikings carefully selected a target before
setting out on raids and always put great emphasis on mental
preparation. Arab and other foreign chroniclers were always
amazed at the rational and methodical nature of the people
from the north, the ones with all the pagan gods. Advanced
strategy, encyclopaedic knowledge of the target and a fanatical commitment to a common goal were combined with
flexibility and improvisation. And after all that planning, the
Vikings were infamous for completely changing their plans in
mid-ocean.

The spiritual life of modern man has lost much of the vibrant
colour of the pagans, yet we still put great value on the concept

that what you believe, what you feel and what you dream are the key to what sort of reality you create for yourself. For someone with courage and creativity, the approach is more important than the target. Dedication and goals have a way of finding each other.

A brand develops much like a person. From birth to vibrant middle age it is exactly the same, only completely different. A person grows, makes mistakes, changes, succeeds. It is absurd to expect a person to be the same at the age of twenty as he was at the age of five. It is equally absurd to expect a brand to remain the same in the first fifteen years of its life.

In 1999, Light My Fire AB was founded in Malmö, Sweden by a veteran entrepreneur and his daughter. The original business idea was to market fire-making equipment for the outdoorsman. The first product was Central American fatwood – high-resin pine sticks that burned long and hot even when wet. Made according to Fair Trade norms, environmentally safe and more effective than normal kindling or even lighter fluid, the product was a dream come true for starting both campfires and barbecues. Their second product was a Swedish invention, FireSteel, a magnesium steel alloy that made extremely hot sparks when struck with a piece of steel – over 3,000 °C (5,432 °F). The two products used together were a winner. *We sell fire* became the company motto and everything was focused on building a one-of-a-kind brand built on innovation, quality and a passionate approach to the outdoors.

Sales grew slowly in the first few years as the company went through the usual ups, downs and life-threatening liquidity problems. Through it all the company held on to its vision of the brand and of itself. The passion of the company attracted both of the authors as well as Joachim Nordwall, an industrial designer with experience from the automotive and home appliance industry. We all put our heads together on how to take the company forward and came up with the same word: plastic.

"We sell fire ... and plastic?"

Yes, somehow it made sense – the fire they sold was as much figurative as literal.

The next product was a completely rethought meal kit, triangular in shape, brightly coloured, positively oozing with Scandinavian must-have design and made entirely of plastic. It also featured a number of firsts such as a sexy one-piece combined spoon, fork and knife – the Spork.

The meal kit strengthened the innovative character of the brand and brought it to department stores, design stores and other non-outdoor venues. The product attracted media coverage and sales picked up. Then something completely unexpected happened – orders came in for just the Spork. In its first year on the market, Light My Fire sold over one million Sporks all over the world. Sporks were turning up everywhere, from museum art shops to gadget stores to Wal-Mart.

The company had gone from Central American wood to Swedish plastic, yet they still sold fire.

One look at Light My Fire's corporate culture and marketing and there's no doubt; it's the same brand, only bigger and better. Just as the chubby 5-year-old bookworm boy grows into a tall 30-year-old professor – both have remained true to themselves by changing.

⋆ 5 ⋆

A few words before we set sail: learn the basics

WE ARE ALL CHILDREN of our age and our cultures, with all the conceptions and misconceptions that come with them. As inhabitants of the early 21st century, we're working wonders with technology, but are clueless about things that many ancient civilizations figured out thousands of years ago. In a sense, we're only just now starting to wipe the dark dust of the middle ages from our clothes.

Vikings would consider much of our world view barbarian. Our concepts of time, money, honour, courage, competition, equality, success and faith would horrify most Norsemen in the same way that their physical violence and substance abuse excesses horrify us.

Many of the following concepts, the Vikings got with their mothers' milk. We have to learn them from scratch.

Time

It's not what you think

In the last hundred years, we've simply forgotten many of the most basic concepts of time. For some strange reason, hubris perhaps, we're under the impression that *everything* happens so much faster today. We're surrounded by lightning-fast digital static – hundreds of TV channels clamour for our attention, thousands of advertisements clamour for our money, millions of sites promise us the world. We all have Word, Excel and Outlook, and process information ten times as fast as our parents did, yet what do we process it into? And how much do we really make? We kid ourselves that because we have shiny new gadgets we have a higher standard of living. We kid ourselves that we're part of a new global economy, where fortunes are made and lost in the blink of an eye. We're online, but out of touch.

It's time to sit down in a comfortable chair in a quiet room and review a few laws of physics, economics and human nature. As this is a book on marketing, we'll concentrate on the concepts that are central to succeeding in the marketplace. (As for other, more philosophical concepts – that's another room, another chair and another book.)

■ **Overnight success takes years**

People do win the lottery, both literally and metaphorically. For the most part, however, any business or social undertaking takes years. Even if the idea is brilliant, the timing perfect and the execution flawless, most undertakings take time – yesterday, today and tomorrow. And of that tiny minority that seem to make it literally overnight, most of them have years of preparation and/or false starts behind them. The moral of the story: be creative, be bold and be patient.

▪ Time management is often counterproductive

Most of us have read them or have probably absorbed them by osmosis – those handy little guides for time management and getting things done. The main premise is usually how to structure tasks and make use of dead time for productive work. Breaking time down into units and making efficient use of every minute is the secret to success.

But this is the worst possible formula for the two biggest drivers of success – creativity and passion. Dead time – on planes or trains, waiting, walking – should be used for anything but efficiency. This is a time for dreaming, being silly, letting your mind wander, being nice to yourself, reading an outrageous book, talking to strange people. Even sleep can be intensely creative if you let it. Dead time is when your creativity is at its highest. But only if you *surrender* to it. This is the time when you will get your best ideas, but only if you put away the frigging Excel spreadsheet. And, please, frequent fliers, lose the laptops. Working on those little trays next to your fellow sardines is not only inefficient, it's an affront to your creative self. Relax, play with the plastic cutlery, check out the legs in the aisle, read, scribble, doodle, sleep loudly and drool. The world will be better for it. And so will you.

▪ Thoughts take time

In her best-selling book, *Ten Thoughts About Time*, Swedish physicist and philosopher Bodil Jönsson talks about learning to accept that we don't think any faster today than a hundred years ago or a thousand years ago. Thoughts do take time – not just the actual thinking, but also the complicated cocktail of emotional, biochemical and subconscious impulses that make creative ideas possible. Give yourself time to think and be creative. Why, she asks, is "thinking" not taken seriously enough to have a voicemail code on her telephone at work? There's a code to tell callers that you're in a meeting, away on business, out to lunch, lecturing, on vacation or out sick, but there is no code for "thinking". A physicist, a philosopher and a writer, someone who gets paid to think, Bodil Jönsson asked her receptionist how callers would react if they were told that Ms Jönsson couldn't come to the phone because she was busy thinking. The receptionist politely explained that people would get angry if they were turned away for something that sounded so "unimportant".

The Vikings had no trouble with the concept of time and they were no smarter than we are. When they swept into English villages, they had been honing their fighting and navigating skills for a lifetime; their ships and arms for generations. They saw no contradiction in making quick decisions and planning for the long term. Their stories were passed down verbally from generation to generation. They always did their homework.

When the Vikings did business in eastern Europe and Russia, they were well prepared and well respected. (And they still are.) They often spoke local languages and were so trusted they were occasionally brought in by various warring tribes to mediate in local disputes. (And they still are.)

For now, get re-acquainted with time. Slowly.

Money

What's more important than money?

> *Money is a good servant, but a bad master*
> – old proverb

Hundreds of things are more important than money. If you're only in it for the money, do us all a favour and do something that's less of a public nuisance than marketing.

Just as the Vikings were no match head-on-head for massive armies and navies, using the Viking approach is less effective for selling mass-market items that offer nothing new. Vikings come in small boats full of big ideas. If you're a big boat pushing a small idea, if you work in a company that's an army, Viking Marketing is probably not for you. (Sorry.)

The Viking method is all about improving the quality of life, bringing a sense of adventure back to entrepreneurship and corporate culture, and making it all pay.

Ironically, the only people who laugh all the way to the bank are those who make money doing something they enjoy or believe in.

Those who overrate the importance of money get surprisingly little enjoyment out of it. The greedy, the stingy and the vicious waste a disproportionate amount of time thinking about the almighty dollar/euro/yen and don't really have that much fun.

It may seem strange to find this sort of attitude in this sort of book, but there are two truths to be reckoned with: a simple one and a paradoxical one. The simple truth is that money is only a small part of succeeding in life. The paradoxical truth is that putting your mind (and heart) to things other than money often pays off.

To those who find these truths unusual, we offer this highly abbreviated list as a sort of global public service.

More important than money – the short version list

In no particular order:

- Children
- Family
- Friends
- Being able to come and go as you like
- Leaving the world a tiny, tiny bit better than when you came
- A relationship full of love and laughter
- Being able to goof-off in direct proportion to the amount of work you do
- Looking forward to going to work
- Looking forward to going home
- Freedom from stupid details
- Knowing that what you do to pay the bills is not killing anyone
- Doing work that promotes health and happiness
- Seeing the larger picture
- Knowing that time is not money. Time is just time. Money is just money. There is no rate of exchange
- Knowing how to save time without wasting life

- Having a good laugh or two every day
- Love & lust and a good book

Size

If you're the biggest, you're probably not the best

At the beginning of the twentieth century, there were two types of cars being more or less mass-produced. One reached speeds of nearly 130 kph (80 mph) with impressive acceleration, could run on half a dozen fuels and emitted only carbon dioxide, soot and water. The other could barely reach 30 kph (19 mph), could only be run on gasoline, and emitted hundreds of noxious pollutants.

The fast, clean car was the Stanley Steamer. The slow, dirty one was the Model T Ford. The Stanley Steamer disappeared without a trace and the Model T went on to define the industry.

The reason is very simple – marketing. The Stanley was marketed to a discerning upper-class target group that had money to spend on an exhilarating hobby. The Model T was, from the very beginning, meant to be something everyone in America could have. Production methods reflected and even powered this vision. As sales went up, the retail price went down. Henry Ford was fanatical about constantly lowering price, even to the point of scavenging his own profit margins. Even his own board threatened to mutiny, but his strategy paid off. In a matter of decades the Model T was both a household word and a household item.

Marketing history is full of similar examples. Quick – what's the most *popular* operating system for a PC? Windows. What's the *best* operating system? Just about anything else.

This *biggest is not best* principle of marketing is good news in two ways. First, it proves that marketing and timing are everything. Secondly, it means that even in markets that seem absolutely closed, there is always an imbalance that can open the way for smaller, faster players. Who is biggest? Great, what have they missed? Who's smallest and why aren't they doing better?

Vikings always find a way in.

Standard of living
We've got good news and bad news: it's declining

While the third world has shown feeble signs of improvement, the standard of living in the western world has been declining for decades. Think about it.

In the 1960s and 1970s, a middle-class Los Angeles family could afford a four-bedroom house in a quiet, don't-have-to-lock-your-doors suburb on *one* salary. The same standard forty years later takes *two* salaries and the doors are locked at night.

In 1968, a Ford Mustang had a base price of around $2,600, a little over a month's salary for a small-company middle management executive making about $25,000 a year. The same executive today makes $80,000, while a Mustang starts at $19,995 – almost *three* months' salary. And when you add higher taxes on the car and subtract higher taxes on his income, the difference in buying power is even higher. If you try this formula for other major expenses such as housing, the picture is even more dire, as the statistics from the USA indicate:

- The average home price, adjusted for inflation, has increased 78 per cent since the early 1960s. (Source: Forbes)
- In the early 1970s, for a typical married couple under 30, the after-tax cost of owning a first home was 12 per cent of the household income. By the 1990s, the after-tax cost of owning the same house had risen to 29 per cent of income. (Source: Joint Center for Housing Studies of Harvard University)
- A 30-year-old man in the early 1970s earned 15 per cent more than his father did at that age. Today's 30-year-old can expect to bring in 25 per cent less than his dad did. (Source: Forbes)
- From 2001 to 2004 alone, the number of households spending more than half their incomes on housing increased by 14 per cent to 15.8 million. (Source: Joint Center for Housing Studies of Harvard University)

But even if you set little store by statistics – after all, they can be crunched in so many creative ways – look at the more qualitative indicators of wealth. In the 1960s, for example, most mothers were at home full time. Today, few of them can afford to be. The word "homemaker" has been replaced by the more luxurious "stay-at-home mother". Women find they have less choice – not due to lack of equality, but for purely economic reasons.

One telling image is a scene in the 1965 film *The Graduate* in which the new college graduate is bombarded by job offers. Forty years later, the same graduate from the same university (University of California, Berkeley) is reading books with titles like *Guerrilla Job Hunting* and *Get That Job You Would Kill for Without Actually Having To* ... .

The bottom line: limitations bring opportunities. What can you do to lower the cost of living or raise its quality? What can you do for the underdog, which includes virtually all of us?

Courage

When Leif Eriksson's expedition crossed the far north Atlantic to America around AD 1000–1001, they had a handful of small open boats. They had no idea whatsoever what lay ahead of them; no maps, no sextants, no cabins, nowhere to shelter from the weather. If you told the Vikings that a Spanish-Italian would make the same journey 500 years later in giant caravel ships, with compasses and sextants and at a toasty-warm Mediterranean latitude, they would hardly have been impressed.

When it comes to sheer physical *and* psychological hardship, few of us know of anyone who has the courage to go through anything even remotely similar to the Viking explorers.

Today, we use the word courage when describing a heterosexual man who dares wear a pink shirt. How things have changed ...

Honour

Vikings who sailed together considered each other brothers in a very literal sense. Any wrong to any one of them would be avenged by any fellow crewman. The murder of a crew member meant a lifelong quest for revenge for the others. So, how do you feel about the people you work with?

Being civilized

If we are infinitely more civilized than the barbarian Norsemen, why do we need reams of paper and hordes of lawyers every time a few thousand dollars change hands? And what about gated communities? No Viking would ever understand how any peaceful society could be frightened of itself.

A sense of humour

According to the US Census Report for 2007, Americans spent an average of 8.5 hours a day watching television, using computers, listening to the radio, going to the movies or reading. Vikings would be appalled and saddened. When Vikings sat down to listen to a poet or a storyteller, the man or woman they listened to was the most talented of a talented people famous for their wit. The experience would move the audience to tears or laughter or both. How much on TV can we say the same of today? And 8.5 hours – Vikings believed in storytelling as a celebration of life, not a replacement.

Bloodshed, yes, but first a little poetry

Poets and storytellers were genuinely revered by the Vikings. The Vikings would be shocked at the contemporary western world's lukewarm attitude towards the literary arts. Our anaemic "isn't it nice" lip service and grants-for-culture mentality would have angered them to ... well, they're Vikings – work it out. The Vikings often listened to poetry for a long time before they put on their helmets to go out and slaughter monks. Verbal skill was not only a part of many physical contests, but even a sport in itself.

Is it any surprise that this culture produced some of the great branding stories of our times?

· 6 ·

Plan your attack

GATHER YOUR ARMS, your head and your heart. It's time to plan your attack.

Here are the tactics of Viking branding, in no particular order. Why no particular order? Because everybody and every attack is different. Use whatever works, but do it Viking.

· 7 ·

Use your weaknesses
to your advantage

ABOUT 200 KILOMETRES NORTH of the Arctic Circle lies the
Swedish village Jukkasjärvi, population 540; winter temperature, as low as –40 °C. For two entire weeks in December, the
sun doesn't rise and, no, there's no Starbucks. The only things
available in any abundant amounts in Jukkasjärvi are snow,
ice, cold and darkness. "So what can we sell?" a few locals
asked themselves and each other one day. The natural answer
was: snow, ice, cold and darkness.

"Perfect!" said Yngve Bergquist; "we'll build a hotel. Out of
ice. So people can experience ... ice!"

This was the beginning of the Jukkasjärvi Ice Hotel, a hotel
built entirely of – you guessed it – ice. Since its beginnings
in 1990, the hotel has grown to 85 rooms and 4,000 square
metres. The hotel is built from scratch every November, and
every room is a unique work of art. Every April, the hotel is
allowed to melt. The hotel is adorned with carved and stained
ice windows, ice chandeliers, ice pillars, an ice bar and world-
class ice sculptures. The hotel features an ice chapel, an ice

cinema and rooms with ice beds. People come from all over the world, paying good money to spend a night or two at a room temperature of just under freezing and sip hot beverages out of hand carved ice cups. And for entertainment, there is a nearby full-scale replica of Shakespeare's Globe Theatre with Shakespeare productions performed in the magical light of the snow and ice architecture and set design. Improvements are made and the hotel grows every time it is rebuilt at the beginning of the season. The Ice Hotel hosts TV and film crews, events and exhibitions.

This is a classic example of the Viking formula for success – finding a different way in, around, through, under, over. Many weaknesses have been turned into sales successes over the years. What's your weakness? Is there something flawed, ugly or boring around you? Great! What are you waiting for?

· 8 ·

Decide which small god to pick on

THROUGHOUT HISTORY PEOPLE have worshipped one true god. Obviously, doing business means staying up to date on who that true god is and what the rules are. Breaking these rules can be fatal.

Yet, in every culture, society and market there are a number of smaller gods. These gods are so old and so small that locals don't give them much thought and follow them mostly out of habit. It's these smaller gods that hold the key to success.

Find a weak god who's getting weaker, and kick his ass.

A banal example: in the US automotive market in the 1950s, 1960s and 1970s there was the God of Automotive Safety Denial (GASD). All American auto-makers followed his commandment: Thou shalt not mention the words *car* and *safety* in the same sentence. The gospel of GASD read that if you start talking about safety you will send a message to consumers that cars are not safe. Through decades of cars with self-igniting gas tanks, splinter bomb windshields and no seat belts, GASD was a strong god. Then came consumer activist heathens like Ralph Nader who showed that GASD was a has-been.

The next step was obvious for a Viking: attack that god. The Swedish car manufacturer Volvo, which has always had safety as a primary selling argument in its home market, made a name for itself in the USA by well-timed blasphemy. In an industry dominated by giant companies many times bigger than itself, Volvo did the unthinkable: it showed cars crashing with lifelike dummies. One commercial even showed a Volvo being driven off the roof of a five-storey building.

The result was that Volvo took a share of the market out of all proportion to their microscopic size. By routing old, tired GASD, the Volvo became synonymous with safety.

At about the same time, another European car maker was going Viking on another small local god: Cars Are Always Beautiful, or CAAB.

A car is always a thing of beauty. No American car-maker would dare even hint that their model wasn't the most amazing piece of design in history. Taboo. The Volkswagen Beetle, whatever its aesthetic characteristics, was completely different from contemporary American cars. Here, a conscious decision was made between appeasing CAAB, which would probably have been difficult, or defying him. The decision became one of the most successful ad campaigns of all time. A satirical campaign that was one of the most entertaining in US history.

"Built to stay ugly for a long time," read the ads. And this was good.

So what are today's small gods in that new market or arena? Human nature and the marketplace see to it that there is a never-ending supply of them.

Old traditions can be so quaint

The Vikings inherited a number of pagan sacrifice rites from their prehistoric ancestors – killing things and hanging them in trees, that sort of thing. These blóts, as they were referred to in Old Norse, occurred at the changing of the seasons or at the winter and summer solstice. Every nine years there was a great blót at the temple at Uppsala. The temple was lined with gold and had three statues – Thor in the middle flanked by Odin and Frey. Thor was armed with a hammer and sword, Odin with a sceptre and Frey, the god of fertility, with a phallus of truly god-like dimensions. For protection from famine or pestilence, you would sacrifice to Thor and for victory in war to Odin, but for a good wedding, Frey was your man.

Outside the temple, the number nine was key – nine males of every kind of creature, including humans, were sacrificed and hung in a nearby grove to buy fertility for the crops and favour from the gods. And then, as the sun set over a grove full of hanging corpses, the singing and drinking would start.

When Christianity finally established itself for good in Scandinavia in the twelfth and thirteenth centuries, a church was built on the site.

· 9 ·

Think small and see the big picture

LIVING IN A SMALL COUNTRY can be a great advantage in today's increasingly interdependent global economy. The smaller the home market, the greater the incentive to export. Small countries often have their eyes to the world and their ears to the ground, listening for opportunities. Small countries are quicker to learn new languages, adopt new technology, faster to put aside their own mindsets in order to understand the mindsets of cultures around them.

If you don't live in a small country, pretend you do. How do people in other countries think? What brands have you bought today that are from a country halfway across the world? And why, with all the talent you have in your own country, were they able to offer a better solution?

This is how many Nordic countries have thought for centuries and it has paid off. A hundred years ago, the Swede Lars Magnus Ericsson took apart Alexander Graham Bell's telephone and said to himself, "There's no reason to buy telephones from the other side of the Atlantic; I know I can build a better one here." And he did. His company, that still bears his name, went on to become one of the most successful telecommunications multinationals in the world, offering solutions that often best those of countries with much larger pools of talent to draw upon and hordes of domestic consumers to sell to.

Iceland, with a population of merely 294,000, has taken the small country ethic to record lengths. In the last few years, Icelandic companies and banks such as Baugur, Kaupthing and The FL Group have emerged as the backers for many takeovers in the UK retail sector. With major holdings in Woolworths, House of Fraser, Hamleys, Karen Millen, Oasis, French Connection and Whittards, Iceland has become a soft-spoken giant in London's cityscape.

The giant got louder when Icelandic billionaire Bjorgolfur Gudmundsson bought West Ham football club for £85 million. What's more, one of the biggest children's television shows in the UK last year was Lazytown, an Icelandic import.

Icelanders are traditionally the wildest of the Scandinavian countries, and are the culture that has retained the strongest living ties with their Viking past. While Sweden's attitude towards their ancestors has gone through various stages of denial, celebration and satire, Iceland has always taken its past to its heart. The Icelandic national identity includes feeling that you are a match for the rest of the world, despite the small size of your country. In a country with a microscopic population, it is easier to be seen and heard. Icelanders, like the original Vikings, feel empowered and know they can make a difference in the world.

Iceland's small size also means that people tend to become dabblers and jacks of all trades, which results in that strange but true paradox, that the more generalists, the better the specialists. A look at the all-time great entrepreneurs, inventors and scientists throughout history supports this. Excelling at a speciality often goes hand in hand with having a wide range of talents in other areas.

All these principles apply equally well to companies. Small companies and companies that think like small companies are the ones with the biggest potential. It used to be that big profits always meant a factory and a skyscraper headquarters. Nowadays, with $20,000 in servers you can play with the big boys.

If you have a big idea and a sneak attack.

· 10 ·

Think big and see the small opening

ONE OF THE VIKINGS' unofficial exports was human DNA. Flings, intermarriages, rapes – the Vikings spread more than just destruction on their voyages all over Europe. Centuries and centuries later, Denmark may well still be the world's leading exporter of human semen.

A small, export-dependent economy, Denmark has always had to look abroad for new opportunities. Looking around for what Danes produce an over-abundance of led Ole Schou to found a sperm bank. In a country where over six per cent of new births involve some form of assisted reproduction, there was a strong tradition of sperm donation. Not only do all men have the option of testing their sperm count in routine health controls, the country has always had a permissive attitude towards sex and a huge percentage of blood donors – a full eight per cent of the population.

By taking a step back and seeing the big picture – new legislation about revealing donor identity and the difficulty in attracting donors – it was easy to see that a sperm bank catering to the European market would be a good idea.

Enter Cryos International Sperm Bank. To date, the company has engendered some 12,000 children since it opened its doors, adding some 1,400 more every year. Semen with five million sperm cells per millilitre sells for €26 per 0.4 ml straw, while the prime stuff with 50 million per millilitre goes for a whopping €264 per straw. At 1–4 straws per treatment and 5–6 treatments per pregnancy, this adds up, and when combined with ancillary services and products, the sales are impressive for such a narrow niche company. *The Times* has referred to the company as being on its way to becoming "Europe's sperm powerhouse."

Aside from the willingness of Danes to give sperm – it's considered in the same category as donating blood – Cryos is also built on a Scandinavian sense of quality, pragmatism and attention to detail. All donors are rigorously tested both for sperm count and for diseases and genetic defects. Only one in ten are accepted and all samples are kept in quarantine for at least six months before being released. The standards imposed on the donors and on the semen handling are making an international name for the company. In the industry, their products are referred to as "the good stuff," and the large number of successful pregnancies bears this out.

The moral of the story: even the smallest of cultural differences can pay off, if you keep your eyes open, think quality, and think long term.

Sex? What, now?

Vikings lived in tight-knit communities and very open households. Foreign visitors were often shocked by other people in the household having sex in the background while they were in the middle of negotiations. Vikings neither understood nor tolerated the strange sexual morals of people from Christian continental Europe. As early as the fifth or sixth century, Viking women were practising birth control based on effective herbal potions. Vikings were probably no more promiscuous than their Christian European counterparts, only happier.

· 11 ·

Even in a war of words, actions speak louder

BOLD IDEAS FOLLOWED BY bold actions are often the best credentials.

At the end of the 1930s, archaeological evidence suggested that Polynesia had been populated by two separate migrations by sea from Asia. A young student, Thor Heyerdahl, claimed otherwise: one of these migrations had come from the other end of the world – South America. He based his theory on his time spent in Polynesia, where he observed many tell-tale similarities. In the jungle of Hivaoa, for example, he had observed stone statues that were identical to those found in Colombia, 6,000 kilometres to the east. This discovery marked the beginning of his controversial theory that the first wave of Polynesians had come not from Asia by canoe, but from South America by balsa wood raft. He met strong resistance from the scientific community. Anthropologists had long been certain that no American type of prehistoric vessel could have brought people to Polynesia alive. Heyerdahl's year living as a primitive on a deserted island in Polynesia had taught him much about the people and the region. He observed that the prevailing currents and trade winds ran from east to west, making it unlikely that the population had arrived sailing against the wind.

What could have gone on for decades as a war of words became instead one of the most famous Viking voyages of modern times. In 1947, Heyerdahl built a balsa wood raft using ancient techniques and named it Kon-Tiki, after the seafaring sun king common to both the ancient Inca kingdom and the islands of Polynesia. The raft left the port of Callào in Peru with six men on board, and after travelling for 101 days and 8,000 kilometres over the open Pacific Ocean, the raft landed on the Raroia Atoll in the Tuamotu Archipelago.

Some scientists refused to believe that the incredible voyage had actually taken place until a documentary film about the expedition was released. The film won an Oscar for best documentary and Heyerdahl's popular book *The Kon-Tiki Expedition* became an international bestseller and was translated into 70 languages.

Heyerdahl went on to study a number of other archaeological puzzles, resulting in a number of other daring voyages – the most spectacular of which was his crossing of the Atlantic in a boat made of papyrus reeds. To date, his books have sold over 50 million copies.

When the Icelandic-born Viking Leif Eriksson set out from Iceland nearly a thousand years earlier, he did more than simply discover North America: he created a tradition of men who think with more than their mind.

Heyerdahl looked back at his heritage with a Viking heart and looked forward with a scientist's soul.

A true Viking, he changed the world with big ideas and a handful of small boats.

· 12 ·

Make money on suffering, despair and poverty

The half wit does not know that gold makes apes of many men.
One is rich, one is poor

– from "Hávamál"

AT THE END OF 2006, more than half of the world's buying power is now in the developing countries. Like most of the really important news, this fact didn't exactly take the world's media by storm. But, it should have.

In 2006, Muhammad Yunus was awarded the Nobel Peace Prize for his work with Grameen Bank in Bangladesh, a bank that makes micro-loans to some of the world's poorest people. Grameen Bank was founded with the help of foreign aid, but quickly became self-financing and *profitable*. The bank helped show the world something unexpected: extremely poor people are very good at repaying loans. In fact, a full 98–99 per cent of the bank's customers repay their loans on time.

Some thirty years after Muhammad Yunus's first loan of $27 dollars to 42 women in a neighbouring village, the bank has lent billions to the country's poor at reasonable rates and made a profit in the process. In 2005, that profit was $15.2 million, almost 20 per cent of their portfolio, according to the bank's website. The scheme has been copied throughout the world: there are now 100 million micro-credit borrowers. Citigroup, Credit Suisse and Dutch bank ABN AMRO have all established micro-banking operations in developing nations with hundreds of local players.

What other opportunities have been missed in developing countries? Those who learn how to look at marketing free from preconceived notions have a head start in these markets.

An idea, a brand and a feel for mutual benefit. The rest is just maths.

· 13 ·

Make money on human decency

WHEN YOU SAY BRANDING, few people think of charitable and cultural organizations. The truth is that these institutions are even more dependent on the power of their brands than private companies.

Cultural and charitable organizations live on their story and the strong emotional attachment it creates. They often have a smaller budget to get the word out.

One brand with a story is that of the Nobel Prizes. When Alfred Nobel, the Swedish industrialist and inventor of dynamite, died in 1895, he willed most of his considerable fortune to the establishment of a foundation to recognize work in the service of humanity. The fortune he had made in a lifetime of marketing explosives and weapons, became the perpetual funding for the Nobel Prizes. In a world of thousands of prizes, many that spend billions promoting themselves, the Nobel Prizes are widely considered the world's most prestigious awards for intellectual achievement.

Here, the product is the brand. Its integrity and wisdom speak for themselves. Astute, sometimes unpopular, sometimes political – the choice of Nobel laureates is often epoch-making and always of a quality that reflects back on the quality of the prizes themselves.

It doesn't take a Nobel Prize laureate to figure out the economics behind an institution that is respected and watched around the world.

There is nothing funny about peace, love and understanding.

Especially if it generates billions in goodwill and export dollars.

· 14 ·

Be humble and rude
(rather than arrogant and polite)

Two wooden stakes stood on the plain,
On them I hung my clothes:
Draped in linen, they looked well born,
But, naked, I was a nobody

– from "Hávamál"

BEING HUMBLE AND RUDE is not only a good rule of entrepreneurship, but also a good social principle.

Creativity is dampened by arrogance and preconceived notions.
Be humble, always.

Change is stifled by fear and a misplaced respect for social
norms. Be rude, sometimes.

"If you can't say anything nice, don't say anything at all" is a
nice way of saying "Shut up and don't rock the boat." Speak
up when things are not as they should be and you'll discover
that there are more people than you think who feel the same.

No human emotion occurs in a vacuum. If you feel something strongly, chances are that you are not alone.

Try thinking like an underdog. Underdogs have nothing to lose and everything to gain, an attitude that makes it much easier to tap into fresh creativity.

You're a Viking four days a week whether you like it or not

The most important territory the Vikings colonized was your mind. In English and the Germanic languages, most of the days of the week are named after Viking gods. Tuesday comes from Tyr, the Viking god of war. Wednesday comes from Odin; Thursday originates from Thor's-day, named in honour of Thor, the god of thunder. Friday was derived from Freyja's-day. Freyja was Odin's wife and represented love, beauty and quite a bit of infidelity in Norse mythology – an inspiration for our modern notions of Friday night, perhaps.

⋆ 15 ⋆

Adopt a target group – people you like or people like you

WHEN YOU STUDY MARKETING, you are taught that marketing is a science (almost) based on a number of solid principles, the most important of these being *the target group*.

In the sterile classroom you examine the concept *target group* at length – by cold fluorescent lights you dissect it, catalogue it, label it and toss it around a little until you get the feel of it. Your mission is to locate a target group and please it.

This is very good thinking, but lacklustre. Marketing should naturally be aimed at the people who have an interest in buying a particular product or service, but marketers tend to leave out a few interesting factors.

First, most marketers are taught to take themselves out of the equation. We have been conditioned to approach things coldly and rationally. "What does the target group want?" we ask ourselves as if we are not part of any target group. We have distanced ourselves so far from the target group that the joy of entrepreneurship and discovery has been removed for both people who sell things and people who buy them. By approaching marketing impersonally, everyone loses. The best companies and products have grown from the preferences of the marketer, not the target group. We have become accustomed to cranking out things and then trying to figure out where to put them. The Viking philosophy turns the target group reasoning around.

A Viking always begins by making himself the target group. He asks himself: What do *I* want personally? What sort of brands and products do I like? What qualities do I respect and which do I dislike? What would make my life better? What do I find annoying?

By putting yourself into the equation, you commit yourself emotionally and it is this emotion that will generate the buzz. A charismatic brand, like a charismatic person, gets noticed not so much for what's on the outside, but what's on the inside. Burn for your brand and your brand will burn for you.

Secondly, don't put too much thought into giving people what they want. They don't know what they want until you show it to them. What's more, everyone – young, old, experienced, naive, open or cynical – wants to be seduced. And you have what it takes to seduce them, whisper sweet nothings in their ear.

It's a rough job, but someone has do it.

PS: A cautionary note about selling to a target group

There is an unconfirmed but very instructive story from when the Vikings landed in Vineland – the Viking word for North America – and made the acquaintance of the Native Americans. The Vikings, having brought a few cows along on the voyage, gave them the gift of milk – something the Native Americans rather liked. Only one problem; it seemed that a great many of them were probably lactose intolerant, and they became very ill. The braves returned to avenge the poisoning and the Vikings, being ridiculously out-numbered, were forced to turn and run.

The moral of the story: Be careful about doing unto others as you would have them do unto you – unless you are sure that what you're doing is something they would have done unto themselves.

· 16 ·

Make money by giving things away

THE MORE THE DIGITAL sector grows, the more money you can make giving things away. Take three modern successes: Google, Skype and YouTube. On Google you get free searches, free advice, free maps, free satellite pictures, free access to millions of photos. You can use it 24 hours a day and it won't cost you a penny. Skype lets you call, chat, email and network all over the world for free, and YouTube is again free, free, free.

All these companies think like Vikings. (But only Skype can claim any Scandinavian connection – one of the founders, Niklas Zennström, is Swedish.) All of them are laying a new mental infrastructure – redefining how we communicate and how we make money. Vikings started with some creative ways of making money. One, *danegeld,* (literally "Danish gold"), was to attack a city and then return to extort money for promising not to attack it again and then ... well, attacking it again. When fortifications, arms and armies improved, making attacks less profitable, the Vikings often turned to trade. They quickly reinvented themselves as businessmen, using the lessons they had learned in their travels and their campaigns. They invested in a new mental infrastructure.

The new mental infrastructure for the 21st century is based on being able to communicate and find information effortlessly. Like physical infrastructure – roads, airports, that sort of thing – mental infrastructure must be so public that it becomes part of our daily lives, a sort of human right. While physical infrastructure only generates income in a very indirect way for those who built it – road taxes, fuel taxes, income taxes on the private sector incomes generated and so on – tomorrow's mental infrastructure will generate revenues directly for those who build it. These revenues will be a complicated mix of click-throughs, rankings, paid listings, multimedia service extras and so on, but they will be substantial, lasting and ever-changing.

Start your contribution today. Give something away. Make a million.

· 17 ·

Start innovative, stick to your principles, change

Just when I discovered the meaning of life, they changed it
– George Carlin

VIKINGS, BUDDHISTS AND BRANDING consultants will all tell you the same thing: the only constant is change. To prosper, you must change with the times, change the times or do a little of both.

Building blocks had been around for thousands of years when Ole Kirk Christiansen founded a Danish company to make ... well, more of them.

Humans had known for centuries that letting children combine blocks freely was great for both their physical and intellectual development. The new Danish company, it would seem, was just another face in the crowd. The year was 1932 and the name of the company was LEGO.

Today, every person on earth has an average of 52 LEGO blocks, according to the company. With a home market of

4 million people, barely the suburbs of New York, LEGO is the sixth largest toymaker in the world. The world's children spend 5 billion hours a year playing with LEGO. Are they all trying to find the 915,103,765 different ways the company claims that six eight-stud bricks can be combined? Or has the company done something very Viking?

The little plastic brick, though very innovative when it was introduced, would have eventually succumbed to competition or pirating if it hadn't evolved. It not only evolved, but often it set the standard for how to play creatively, how to let children tell their own stories.

The Danes have always had a strong storytelling tradition that is so universal that most people don't even know that the stories are Danish. Perhaps the best-known fairy tales in the English language are those of the nineteenth-century Dane Hans Christian Andersen: "The Ugly Duckling", "The Little Mermaid", "The Emperor's New Clothes" and "The Princess and the Pea", to name just a few.

LEGO has a similar kind of universal storytelling appeal. Simplicity with constant variation, constant new twists. A look at the development of the little plastic block is dizzying. From adding motors and gearboxes, to figures, to computer-operated robots – all this before the end of the 1980s.

Through licensing agreements with such creative players as Lucasfilm, the brand has associated itself time and time again as a friend of the great story.

The plastic blocks have even continued to prosper in the digital age, with a website that is one of the most popular family sites in the world today. According to the company, LEGO.com attracts 6,308,558 visitors per month who stay an average of seven minutes per visit.

The company has had its ups and downs over the years, but if they continue to keep the new twists coming, they will be a force to be reckoned with for a long time to come.

Relearning technology

When scientists first started to build copies of Viking longboats, they were disappointed and confused. The ships seemed far too fragile to have made the voyages they made. They eventually discovered some new-old technology: Vikings had an ingenious way of using the direction of the wood's grain in their nautical designs. By taking great care to ensure that the grain ran in the same direction as the curve of the piece it was to be used for, the strain was put against the grain, where the wood is the strongest. What's more, the longboat design allowed the ship to flex with the movement of the water – another modern eighth-century innovation.

· 18 ·

Blend in by standing out

CONVENTIONAL WISDOM FOR BRAND-BUILDING is to create a single profile, a single personality that is consistent all over the world. This makes good sense and there are many examples of brands that look, feel and talk the same everywhere.

One of the Vikings' biggest strengths, however, was their willingness to learn from other cultures. When they returned to the north after their voyages through the continent, the British Isles, the Mediterranean and the Byzantine Empire, they brought back as much culture as cargo. When they settled abroad, as they often did, they learned the language and quickly blended in. Today's Normandy was once heavily populated by the Normans, descendants of Vikings. The Normans left a huge footprint by conquering large parts of Europe and, at the Battle of Hastings, subduing the Saxons and changing the history of England.

On the one hand, the Viking brand was so strong, so consistent and so forcefully communicated that it managed to outlive the product – the Vikings themselves – by a thousand years. The Viking brand succeeded on its own terms, yet was very chameleon in other cultures. Is this a contradiction? Can a brand both stand out and blend in?

Of course. Here are two cases.

Quick, what's the world's third most read newspaper? *New York Times*? The *Sunday Times*? *Dainik Jagran*? *Yomiuri Shimbun*? Try again. It's a Swedish paper: *Metro*. What??

Metro was launched in Stockholm in 1995 as a new approach to newspapers. It was distributed free of charge on public transport designed for a "twenty-minute" commute-read, with short articles tailored to the tastes of a young, urban audience. This audience was disenchanted with traditional newspapers and had long been written off by many newspapers. A Viking dream come true, the equivalent of an unguarded monastery – an abandoned target group. *Metro* quickly produced local editions for cities all over Sweden and became a phenomenon in the business with profit margins unheard of in the newspaper industry. This in itself would have been a Viking accomplishment, a tactical invasion of an unguarded port. In the classic Viking mode, however, the paper quickly went abroad, using the same layout, name, philosophy and energy in city after city, country after country. In each new market, the look and feel was the same, the philosophy was the same, the attitude and the brand the same, but the content was produced by local reports and local wire services. In ten years, the paper grew to 64 editions in 91 major cities in 19 countries and 18 languages in Europe, North America, South America and Asia. The paper from the tiny country of Sweden with 9 million inhabitants is read by 18.5 million people a day and 37 million readers a week in 2006. That put it just behind *Dainik Jagran* and *Dainik Bhaskar* in India, with 21.2 and 21 million readers respectively.

Another example is the granddaddy of all reality soaps: *Robinson*. If the name doesn't ring a bell, don't be surprised; you probably know it by the name of *Survivor*. Charlie Parsons of Bob Geldof's production company Planet 24 came up with the idea, but was unable to sell it to English or American TV and eventually approached Strix Television in Sweden, who became the first in the world to produce his concept as *Expedition Robinson*. The programme was a runaway hit – one episode was watched by over 4 million viewers, about half the country's population. The programme was then exported to the rest of the world and has since been made in dozens of countries. The format is the same in every market, yet different.

The Swedish production company Strix still produces or co-produces a number of the international versions in fourteen countries.

Who would have thought of launching a TV concept just south of the Arctic Circle? Burbank, Hollywood, London – yes. Stockholm, hardly.

Regardless of what you may think of the concept, it's a modern phenomenon. And a Viking sneak attack.

· 19 ·

Learn the new maths

An economist who is just an economist can never be a
good economist

– Vernon L. Smith, 2002 Nobel Laureate, Economics

PHILOSOPHY is often the best mathematics.

The American Henry David Thoreau argued in 1854 that it was *faster* to walk ten miles (16 kilometres) than it was to take the train. He reasoned that buying a ticket to go ten miles on the train cost $1, about a day's work at minimum wage. While the person travelling by train is still at work making the money to pay his fare, the walker has already covered the distance. The walker has arrived a day before the worker; he has covered the distance more than eight hours *faster*. Every journey begins with the time it takes to pay for it.

The price-specific elements of this argument don't hold up with modern equivalents – a ten-mile journey on a train costs closer to one hour's work than one day's work – but the approach is as applicable as ever. If you want to find out what things really cost, you have to look at the larger picture.

A good way to start thinking Viking is to use variations of this kind of philosophical mathematics. Let's look at the real mathematics behind software piracy, for example.

As people who make a living on intellectual property, the authors are less than thrilled by the morals of stealing software. Yet, moral or immoral, software piracy is often as profitable for the software makers as for those who use the software for free.

Let's take an example everyone with a computer can relate to: Microsoft Word. About 15–20 years ago, Word cost many times more than today, even when adjusted for inflation. Let's say at that time that there were ten people who wanted to buy Word, but only ten per cent of them could afford it – one person. That one person bought it and let the other nine copy it for free. Those friends each gave it to ten people, bringing the Word community to 100 users. When the next version of the program was released it was still only purchased by ten per cent of those who wanted it, but now, with 100 users, that ten per cent was not one person but ten people. As this viral process rolled on, pretty soon there were millions of users, and even with only ten per cent paying for the product, this still meant hundreds of thousands of buyers. The major development costs for the product had long since been recouped, and the unit price of the program began to drop, with the result that the ten per cent of those buying the program rose to twenty per cent, and what's more, that twenty per cent was no longer in the thousands but in the millions, with the program firmly established as the world standard. And it all started with nine pirated copies.

This formula works on different levels and in different ways for all intellectual property that is used repeatedly and can be upgraded or followed up with a "sequel" – music, film, books.

So, should you allow people to steal your intellectual property? Not if you can help it, but you must also be sensitive to the shifts in mathematical philosophy that a new digital age brings.

Now that the dotcom hysteria has vanished without a trace, you can watch those who are making money on new philosophies that are challenging and changing our concepts of democracy and business.

And watch for blasphemous new ideas that are making money.

A novel novel

An unlikely combination of I, Claudius and Monty
Python, the two-volume Swedish novel Röde Orm ("The
Long Ships") by Frans G. Bengtsson, first published between
1941 and 1945, is probably both the funniest and most
historically accurate piece of storytelling about the Vikings
ever written. From trying to understand Christianity
("What you're saying is that he's a God and he gets nailed
to a piece of wood. I don't get it ... "), to beer-soaked sword
fights and Mediterranean slavery, the book follows the fate
of a kind of Viking Everyman, Röde Orm, who experiences
everything that Vikings experienced collectively in the two
hundred years that they were at their height – feasts, poetry,
battle and business.

· 20 ·

Perfect the product

THE TECHNIQUES OF MARKET communications have become so refined that the phrase "we can sell anything" is more or less taken for granted. In most books on marketing and advertising, 99 per cent of the focus is on how to make yourself heard in the marketplace. Actually creating something to sell is considered beside the point.

Get back to basics. Commit yourself to making the best possible product or service. Ask yourself "How will this improve the quality of life of whoever buys it? Will it help him/her pursue a dream, find meaning, live longer, be healthier or have an extra hour or two of freedom? Is it good for a laugh or even just a smile?"

There are so many products that shouldn't even be on the market. The myth is that no one is forced to buy a certain product. But if you're hungry, what do you do if the only restaurants available to choose from are fast-food chains? If you're thirsty, what do you do if the drinking fountain has been replaced by a soft drink machine? In a supermarket, finding wholesome bread or breakfast cereal can be almost impossible. As a consumer you have been fooled into thinking that having a choice between a great multitude of similar products is the same as freedom.

This fake choice dilemma has been made possible by a certain amount of corruption and complacency on both sides of the consumer/corporation equation. Huge conglomerates have pushed out smaller players while consumers have been too lazy to protest.

This is bad news and good news. People don't know what they want, but somewhere inside there is always a latent longing for honesty and quality. This hunger doesn't always show up in market research, which means that it's a golden opportunity.

People don't know it, but they are dying for real products.

And dying for someone to help bring them back to reality.

· 21 ·

If your product is really terrible, spend your marketing money on the product

ONCE UPON A TIME there was a country that was seen by most of the world as aggressive, with appalling human rights abuses. A famous brand consultant was brought in to clean up what even the country's staunch supporters saw as a tarnished image.

The consultant had made heroes out of tobacco companies and health food gurus out of fast food chains. They knew he was their man and they could immediately ask all the right questions.

"What do you think? Commercials, cultural events, celebrity tours? Who should we use as a spokesman? What do you think we should do?"

"Will you think about what I have to say?" the brand man asked.

"Why of course, you're a legend."

"Release half your prisoners, distance yourself from these six dictators, write off these three loans and quadruple your foreign aid budget. Then I'll write a few press releases for free."

The government men took notes, asked to hear more on each point and then thanked him for his time. The next week the man behind a phenomenal chocolate chip cookie brand was called in. A celebrity spokesman was chosen and untold millions were poured into what was touted as "The Campaign of the Century".

A year later, the campaign had been forgotten and the image was still tarnished. The moral of the story is that even with unlimited resources and talent, the product is still of primary importance. A terrible product is difficult to sell.

· 22 ·

There are millions of products but only two brands – be both of them

IN OUR LIFETIMES we'll see or own tens of thousands of products and be bombarded with countless brands. But, in reality all brands boil down to two emotional concepts: meaning and entertainment.

Products come with rational arguments; brands are all built on a simple emotional attraction. This attraction comes down to *meaning* and *entertainment*. Is there something in this brand that will make me smile (entertainment), fit in (meaning), attract the opposite sex (meaning and entertainment – you decide the relative proportions ...), make me feel safe (meaning), make me feel at home (meaning), give me something to do in the afternoon (entertainment), let me express myself (meaning or entertainment or both) ... ?

But only two? Yep.

Think about this story. A Chinese traveller met a British traveller and through an interpreter they compared each other's cultures. One thing led to another and pretty soon they were comparing literature and writing.

"In China," said the Chinese traveller, "we have such a rich literary tradition. Why, we have over a hundred thousand symbols. How many do you have in English?"

"Twenty-six."

"Twenty-six?"

"Yes ... "

"How can you ever write anything of any subtlety with only twenty-six symbols?"

Ah, but we can.

And how could Mozart write such beautiful music with only eleven notes in the classical chromatic musical scale? Ah, but he could.

This text is being written on a digital machine that can only think in two symbols: 1 and 0. But we all know what computers can do.

Meaning and *entertainment* are the zeros and ones of branding. Like software applications, these long series of zeros and ones form a whole that works either well or badly.

0 The total meaning/entertainment content determines the *power of the brand*

1 The relative proportions of the two determine the *personality of the brand*

Try them out on brands you admire. For example:

Apple

Total entertainment and meaning content	*Sky high content of both.* Lots of entertainment – iWhatever to the X power. And lots of meaning – this is not an operating system, it's a cult. It's also a creative tool to help make your dreams come true – web fame, the breakthrough film, the hit song, the killer podcast.
Relative proportions	*70 per cent entertainment* – let's face it, the nice graphics/applications are a gas to use, but a PC can do more or less the same thing with a lot more third-party applications to chose from.
	30 per cent meaning – yes, it is inspiring and the cult is warm and welcoming.

Greenpeace

Total entertainment and meaning content	*Moderately high to high.* Once very high, but with in-fighting, hints of scandals and the mainstreaming of their message, the brand does not have the charisma it once had.
Relative proportions	*70 per cent meaning* – What can be more important than saving the world?
	30 per cent entertainment – Let's face it, the ads are clever and their Zodiacs make for much better TV than anything Jacques Cousteau ever gave us.

Try it out on your own brand.

Should you change the relative proportions? Should you be more of one or more of the other? Do you need more of both?

You decide, but stay real.

· 23 ·

Competition is a secondary consideration

I'd rather win a bronze medal than a silver one. A silver medal means you are the best of all the losers. The No. 1 loser

– Jerry Seinfeld

COMPETITION MEANS WINNING at the expense of others. Only one can win, while everybody else loses. On a personal level, in an organization or in a society, competition is not just unpleasant, it's unnecessary and counterproductive.

Both common sense and hundreds of studies, clinical and cross-cultural, have shown time and time again that competition does not produce excellence, nor does it foster creativity. In fact, in education, research, the arts and business, it is clear that competition produces lower quality, poorer performance and less innovation than cooperation in any group setting. (More about this in Part II.)

Let's start at a common-sense level. Suppose you have 100 people in a room where a flash-fire breaks out. Everyone races towards the exit at the same time. In a terrifying 4 minutes and 38 seconds of kicking, fighting and biting, 20 get out and 80 die of smoke inhalation.

Then suppose you have the same fire in a room full of people who have been trained in how to stay calm and work together as rationally as possible. The people in this room file out quickly and calmly. Everyone gets out alive.

In the first room, we have the kind of competitive people who succeed at any cost, people whom many societies worship as heroes: politicians, athletes, gameshow hosts. In the other, people who are used to working together, people who have some sort of notion that if everyone participates, everyone comes out ahead.

In one room there are winners and corpses. In the other, there are only winners.

Doing business, we're told, is the first room. If we don't move faster than everyone else, we'll die in the smoke and fumes. Only twenty people can get out of the exits, we're told. The rest must die.

In a room, we easily see the fallacy of this reasoning, but not in our everyday lives nor in the business world. To make things worse, in this comparison there is only one exit; in business, there are as many as we ourselves create.

True, businesses do cut each other's throats on a daily basis, just as people murder each other and nations go to war, but the day of a successful businessman is far more concerned with making his own business work than with seeing to it that others fail. Trying to succeed and trying to beat others are two different things. People who are preoccupied with winning are less focused on the task in hand and rarely do better work.

In the USA, when someone is called "competitive", it is meant as a compliment. Phrases such as "he's a real competitor," "he's got killer instinct" and "she's going to win or die trying" are accepted without a thought as something positive.

In many countries, however, these sorts of descriptions would be considered negative and insulting. In Sweden, for example, children are measured by "how well they work in a group" and group activities are more the norm than the exception. In Japan, children are encouraged to work together rather than against one another.

In a dog-eat-dog world, quite often it's *not* the dogs that come out ahead. This is considered common sense in many countries and readers there will have to forgive us for kicking in open doors in this chapter. As for the other countries, the USA in particular – wake up and smell the coffee.

· 24 ·

The tools remain the same

WHEN THE VIKINGS SET OFF, they had more or less the same tools as everyone else – swords, ships, shields, spears. The key to their success was how, when and where they used them.

Getting out the word about a new product or idea is based on some very traditional tools – advertising, PR, events, word of mouth, demographics and other buzz words from Marketing 101A. The key is how, when and where they are used.

Going Viking is all about using what you have differently.

· 25 ·

Advertising doesn't work,
and why this is good

Fairest we speak when falsest we think
– from "Hávamál"

INFLATION IS A VERY simple concept: the more of something you produce, the less it's worth. With the growth of the media, the impact of the TV and radio spot has diminished both in visibility and credibility. And remember when you had actually heard of most of the periodicals in the rack of your neighbourhood grocery store? It seems the world has turned into a virtual swamp of information we didn't ask for and have no interest in.

We spend far too much of our time knee-high in bullshit.

A hundred years ago, when there was relatively little advertising, you merely needed to show your product to sell it. Fifty years ago it was enough to be slightly entertaining or informative. Today, well … I have some bad news and some good news.

The bad news is that a few million dollars of TV time will buy you next to nothing in brand-building. The good news is that for a few thousand you can conquer the world. If you have a good story.

In fact, there is an unwritten rule in branding: the better the story, the less you have to spend on buying media. If the story is good enough, it will attract media attention and word of mouth. If your brand is new, it will make news, and news is free (or at least cheap).

The more newsworthy a brand, the easier the marketing and advertising.

· 26 ·

A good story is worth millions more than it used to be

VIKING SAGAS WERE ALMOST entirely a verbal tradition, preserved at the end of the Viking Era in a handful of written accounts. Though very literate, with a well-developed written language, the Vikings never saw written history and literature as especially important. Vikings created stories, but never wrote them down. Nor did they leave any cities, any monuments, any architecture or religious relics behind. There are no Viking tourist attractions, there are no Viking rides at Disneyland. Yet, Viking culture and mythology are almost as well known as Greek and Roman mythology, both of which came from thousand-year empires recorded in thousands of books. The days of the week are still named after Viking gods, English, German and French are full of Norse words, and millions of people are standing in line to see the latest *Lord of the Rings* sequel, a story inspired by Viking mythology. There are fewer historical Viking remnants than for many civilizations that have disappeared completely, yet the Vikings live on.

The reason is very simple: they make a good story. Closely after the primal physical needs of man – food, water, sex and territory – come the inner needs. One of the most important is the pursuit of happiness and meaning – putting yourself in a story that makes sense, hopefully with a happy ending. Literature, music, art, history, religion, psychology and philosophy all make noble attempts to bring order to the chaos of the human world. Every flash of wit or profundity is worth its weight in gold. Those minutes when the universe suddenly makes just a little more sense are what we all live for.

A good story has primal power that goes beyond words. Its truth is in its power and its power is in its truth. A good story moves mountains, creates religions, countries, fortunes.

Success doesn't just come from giving the world a good idea, product or service; it comes from giving it a great story, a story that lives on all by itself.

What's your story? And how do you tell it? Think long and hard; there could be millions at stake.

How much is a wife worth?

" ... 36 marten furs for a good farmer's daughter in her prime, healthy and strong without physical defects or handicaps. The furs must be of the best winter quality, free from damage or arrow holes; or 30 beaver skins in equally good condition ... and a new linen shift, a horn comb, three needles with eyes and a pair of scissors."

A hearing to settle a dispute on how to reimburse an old widow for her two daughters who had left home to marry two strangers without her permission. From the novel Röde Orm *("The Long Ships") by Frans G. Bengtsson.*

· 27 ·

Viking Zen
(or summer fashion at 30 below zero)

IF A TREE FALLS in the forest and no one hears it, is it good marketing?

The answer, of course, is yes. The phenomenon is called Viking Zen.

A case in point is the outdoor clothing manufacturer, Patagonia. In the 1980s and into part of the 1990s, Patagonia donated ten per cent of its net profits to small grassroots environmental movements. The donations were never made public, were never mentioned in press releases or glossy corporate brochures. This policy was maintained for well over a decade, resulting in millions of dollars invested in effective environmental activism.

While auto companies and oil companies spent billions to advertise microscopic environmental contributions, Patagonia spent millions and remained quiet. Was this noble? Of course. Was this good business and good PR? You bet.

Even though Patagonia shunned PR, the recipients of the funding talked to friends, to family, to neighbours, who talked to friends, family, neighbours. Word spread in precisely the right target group for Patagonia's products – people with outdoor interests – and Patagonia's sales skyrocketed. The company has since made its programme public, but still retains the highest credibility.

Another pioneer of Zen PR is Absolut Vodka. In the early days, with its very limited ad budget, Absolut created clever and bizarre ads that appeared in publications with limited, but avant-garde readership. The original ads generated talk and editorial coverage that reached millions. As the brand grew and increased its budget it still used the same Zen PR tactics, only on a larger scale. Spending untold millions, Absolut commissioned designer Versace to create summer fashions for supermodels such as Kate Moss and Naomi Campbell to model outdoors in winter in northernmost Sweden. A set of stunning pictures was taken by the legendary Herb Ritts in a setting of snow and ice near the Jukkasjärvi Ice Hotel. The temperature: 30 below zero. The models were photographed for a few minutes at a time in the arctic cold, then quickly wrapped in blankets and taken into a heated tent to recover before the next few minutes out in the cold. This strange big-budget production resulted in classic photographs that were used in an insert in *Elle*. With a circulation of just 400,000, this was probably the most expensive per head advertising in history. Was it smart to spend so much money to reach so few people? Of course. Within six months, these photos had been seen by almost a billion people around the world in editorial articles in everything from Sunday papers to photography magazines.

Zen PR. Do something that is honest, honourable and interesting. Then don't tell anyone about. Remember: a good story can never be kept secret.

· 28 ·

Go against type

A GOLFER HAS WHITE SHOES, a new car and is usually approaching or passing middle age, or so the stereotype goes. Many golfers fit this image, many don't. If you were in an organization that needed to promote golf, a good strategy would be to move away from this stereotype without offending the many golfers that more or less correspond to it.

But how?

A good branding consultant would begin with two words: Alice Cooper. Alice Cooper, the legendary rock musician known for decades for outrageous stage shows, spitting blood, biting the heads off birds – all the cult Viking sorts of things – just happens to be a fanatical golfer. He is great friends with half a dozen very famous golfers and his game is just shy of professional.

Alice Cooper, with his running mascara, blood-smeared make-up and maniacal poses, would be the dream poster boy and spokesman for giving golf a younger, edgier personality. And older, squarer golfers, having grown up with him and his music, would relate to the nostalgia factor – Alice Cooper hasn't been considered threatening for twenty years.

And the idea could be replicated.

"Golfer" reads the caption over a picture of Ozzy Osbourne or any one of a dozen other personalities/golfers that go against type. "Profession: TV family. Handicap: Probably."

Messages that slightly jar our world-view or common sense stick with us. People who surprise us often win our hearts.

Some years ago, Bob Geldof interviewed Nelson Mandela. When it came to the subject of music, he asked him what sort of music he preferred.

"A lot of types," he answered.

"What, blues and jazz?" Geldof coaxed.

"Oh, no."

"Rap, soul?"

"No."

"Rock and roll?"

"No."

"Classical?"

"Once in a while, but you know what I really like? That Swedish group ... Abba!"

Who would have guessed it, the quintessential African leader an Abba fan.

The world is a strange place. Let's do what we can to keep it that way.

· 29 ·

Use education as marketing

WHEN ABSOLUT STARTED the Absolut Akademi in the early 1990s, it was a attempt to test the effectiveness of using education as direct marketing. The Akademi would educate key people within the organization and outside about vodka in general and Absolut in particular. Journalists, bartenders, cultural personalities were invited to Åhus in southern Sweden for an entertaining and intensive course in vodka and a taste of the culture behind it.

To date, over 100,000 people have attended the Akademi which has generated thousands of articles around the world and tens of thousands of word-of-mouth soundbites.

If you have a quality product, the rule of thumb is, the more people you get into the act, the more coverage you get in the press and the more buzz you get in the coffee room. This is even true for your own coffee room – the more enthusiastic your own people are about the company, what it produces and how it produces it, the more favourably they talk about it with each other – raising morale – and with others outside work – creating powerful word of mouth. ("I heard it from a guy who works there … ")

PART II

CORPORATE CULTURE

Gebo, the seventh letter of the earlier 24-letter Viking alphabet. It means gift, love, partnership and generosity.

The two lines, just as two lives, begin as solitary journeys. It isn't until they meet that meaning is created. Each remains separate, yet connected.

It is this sort of bond that should be at the heart of all good corporate culture. The Viking ethic: hard work, mutual gain, creativity and teamwork.

How do you build this kind of corporate culture?

PRINCIPLES

· 30 ·

Pillaging, plundering and other family values

WHAT HAPPENED TO VIKING family values – swooping down on a badly defended monastery full of gold, silver and antiquities, plundering all your boats can hold and sailing home rich men? And the perks: carrying off the nicest looking wenches, thrashing the local knights, being your own boss, flexible hours? If nice guys really do finish last, the Vikings were true winners.

Today's Scandinavian countries are peaceful parliamentary democracies with low violent crime rates, strict gun-control, a sky-high standard of living and progressive social welfare.

How does a culture go from producing violent, drug-crazed pirates to hard-working, law-abiding liberals? Modern Sweden, for example, has become such a caring-sharing-sensitive kind of place that teenagers are allowed to get divorced from their parents. How can a culture change so completely?

As we've mentioned before, the answer is that the changes aren't as big as they would appear. Over their thousand-year history, Vikings have succeeded in reducing much of the bloodshed normally associated with corporate culture.

In the following chapter, we will lay the basic principles for a corporate culture that is both humane and profitable.

· 31 ·

Everyone's in charge

IN THE TENTH CENTURY, a group of French delegates were in Denmark and saw a group of Vikings in a boat out on the water.

"What is the name of your leader?" they shouted at the boat.

"He has no name!" came the answer.

"How can this be?"

"Because we're all equal."

In a time of feudalism and despotism, this was a radical concept, centuries ahead of its time. While the rest of Europe had fallen into political chaos marked by endless wars and petty conflicts between local chieftains, the Vikings managed to pull together, not as a nation, but as small groups of close-knit "teams". The Vikings certainly had their fair share of feuding, but they also had a deeply rooted tradition of working together toward a common goal.

The Nordic countries had limited farmland and a harsh climate and the Vikings were forced to look overseas to better their lot. A tour abroad on a longboat was a good way for a landless, low-born Viking to make his fortune. Plundered booty was shared and the entire crew enjoyed the fruits of their labours. Vikings were great believers in the concept that later became known as "the self-made man".

Vikings were soon doing business with half the known world and they earned a reputation for being honest, hard-working merchants with good products. The Viking organization is built on the concept that the freer someone is to speak his mind, the more likely he is to use it.

Long before management theory, the Vikings knew that democracy means empowerment and empowerment means passion and commitment. Democracy is not just a nice theory, it is efficient business.

We all spend most of our waking lives at work. Make the workplace work, make it more human. Ironically, in a positive atmosphere people spend less time thinking about their conditions and more time finding creative solutions to the challenges your organization has before it. Whatever time is lost in the decision-making process will be more than made up for in the jump in productivity, efficiency and innovation.

Countries that have lax employee protection laws would at first glance seem to have an easier time in the marketplace. Companies can easily get rid of employees that don't fit into the organization, whereas in many European companies, especially in the Scandinavian countries, labour regulations make it very difficult to fire people.

Upon closer examination, however, there is another dynamic at work. Job security is a major factor in quality, innovative work. People in Scandinavian companies, for example, are much better at speaking their minds than their counterparts in other countries because there is less risk to your career in having an unpopular opinion. There is nothing more inefficient in an organization than having to play politics.

Power to the people means power to the organization.

· 32 ·

Learn to make the right mistakes

BJÖRN IRONSIDES had a lot to live up to. His father Ragnar Lodbrok had helped lead 120 Viking longboats up the Seine to plunder Paris in AD 845.

So, in 859, Björn left his base on the Loire River in France with 62 ships and set sail for the Mediterranean.

For two years he and his men plundered dozens of cities in France and Italy including Narbonne, Nimes, Valence, Pisa and Fiesole. In 860, their boats heavy with gold and silver, they were ready for the biggest prize of all: Rome. From the first sighting of the city they knew they could not take it by sheer force. They needed a plan.

Björn sent a messenger to the city with a story no Christian ruler could resist – the Viking leader was dying and his last wish was to convert to Christianity. The request was granted, and he was received into the city and baptized into the faith. Shortly after, he died. As a Christian, he was given a proper Christian burial attended by a delegation of Björn's men. As the Viking's body was being lowered into the grave, the corpse sprang to life and thrust his sword deep into the bishop in charge of the ceremony. Björn threw swords to his men from a stash in the coffin, signalling a savage attack on everything that moved. The gates of the city were opened and the rest of Björn's men poured in to rape, ransack and burn the city to the ground.

The booty, as one could imagine, was huge; the operation was a great victory. Only one problem: it was the wrong city. Instead of having conquered the eternal city, they had destroyed an insignificant town called Luna, located between Genoa and Pisa.

The moral of the story is clear: with a bit of courage, conviction and strategy, even mistakes can be profitable. A good idea and solid values are half the journey, the rest is just geography.

Viking graffiti

It seems the Vikings were naughtier than we had at first thought: they wrote graffiti all over the Mediterranean. A handful of recent discoveries reveal rune inscriptions where they shouldn't be: on an ancient stone lion's head from Piraeus in Greece, and in the Hagia Sofia mosque in Istanbul.

The graffiti was usually heroic in nature; for example, a tribute to a lost comrade. Kilroy was still centuries away.

◆ 33 ◆

Problems are a manager's best friend

We've always transformed problems into possibilities. When we start running low on problems, I start to get worried

– Ingvar Kamprad, founder of IKEA

IT COMES AS NO SURPRISE to anyone that necessity is the mother of invention, yet so many companies ignore necessity or fail to learn from it. Just as future pilots are told in flight school that turbulence is your best friend, managers should meet problems head-on as a way to fine-tune a company's business concept, improve efficiency, encourage innovation or improve the brand. It is by taking a close-up look at what is going wrong that we can make things "go better".

In 1956, Gillis Lundgren, one of IKEA's founding fathers, was standing with a colleague, peering into the boot of a car. He had a problem he had encountered before: he couldn't get the bulky wooden table in his hands into the boot. Suddenly he said the historic words: "Oh God, then, let's pull off the legs and put them underneath." IKEA had just given birth to its first flat pack – a concept that was to become a modern mantra and a worldwide phenomenon. The flat pack became an essential part of the mix that would work miracles to bring furniture prices down. It eliminated the cost of shipping vast quantities of air whenever a product was sent from factory to shop or showroom, and it shifted the expensive and labour-intensive work of assembly on to the customer. A small problem became a big opportunity.

Not too many years later, IKEA was faced with a much bigger problem that resulted in an even bigger opportunity. When the Swedish furniture industry saw that this little upstart from the middle of nowhere was underselling them by ridiculous margins, they banded together to put the company out of business. All the furniture retailers and wholesalers systematically intimidated IKEA's furniture suppliers – if you sold to IKEA, you were blacklisted from selling to anyone else in the industry. Founder Ingvar Kamprad was personally banned from all trade shows. Industry-friendly journalists wrote scathing articles about the company. The witch-hunt was on.

As IKEA continued to grow, its suppliers dwindled. Things looked desperate. IKEA was forced to look abroad for manufacturing. In the 1960s and 1970s, the natural place to go was Poland, a stone's throw across the Baltic. Its combination of planned economy price structure and its centuries of furniture-making tradition proved to be an ideal solution to the company's woes. The company negotiated with the government and found a number of suppliers that were re-equipped with new machinery for making IKEA's flat pack products. This created a model that would be repeated in various combinations for decades to come, ensuring that IKEA's products would always be much, much less expensive than anything else on the market.

Two problems became more than just two opportunities, but an entire industry.

Who knows what your problems can do for you?

· 34 ·

Put berserkers in the front of the boat (… but don't let them steer)

berserker: an ancient Scandinavian warrior frenzied in battle and held to be invulnerable. The origin of the word "berserk" in English and a number of other languages

THE VIKINGS STRUCK without warning and without mercy. The monks who provided most of our eyewitness accounts characterized them as demons with insane strength that could come only from one source – the devil.

Much of this terror was no doubt created by the *berserkers*, special Viking warriors known for their frenzy in battle. The berserkers sat in the front of the boat, often foaming at the mouth and literally chewing on their shields with wild anticipation at the thought of battle. They were often bigger than your average Viking, who in turn was head and shoulders taller than most of the people he plundered. In battle, berserkers felt neither pain nor fear and seemed to have super-human strength. Naturally, the drugs helped. Berserkers were particularly fond of powdered fly agaric, which not only produced a hallucinogenic high, but also had a certain steroid effect, increasing strength, stamina and prowess in battle.

It was natural, therefore, to let the berserkers sit in front of the boat and jump ashore first. The Vikings were fierce, the berserkers terrifying. There are accounts of berserkers continuing to fight despite severed limbs and life-threatening wounds.

Of course, armed, six-foot psychotics on drugs aren't all fun and games. Even the Vikings were divided on the subject. Berserkers could cause all sorts of trouble on long journeys across the North Sea. Some could become so frenzied that they jumped off ship for no reason in the middle of the ocean. Others ran amok on social occasions when the beer and mead flowed freely.

One thing was agreed, however: don't let the berserkers steer the boat.

In today's business world there is nothing to be gained from psychotic violence (unless of course you're preparing for a career in politics). Yet every organization can put the principle of the berserker to use. In every organization there are a few people who don't quite fit.

They can be anything from eccentric to careless to dissident. Normally, they are neutralized or marginalized and their input is either censored or buried.

Remember, however, most successful organizations are founded by eccentrics. Howard Hughes, Henry Ford and Thomas Edison were all more or less wild and all more or less strange. This spirit is quickly lost as an organization grows larger and more cautious. To stay successful, an organization must make use of its berserkers. The software guy who spends more of his working time developing games than seeing to the corporate enterprise system; the stand-up comedian secretary with the razor sharp tongue; the old senior management guy who you keep out of customer meetings for fear that he'll make a crack about the company or tell a joke about animals – these people often have the creative energy to take your organization to new heights.

The new berserkers: encourage them, listen to them, bring them on board. But again, don't let them steer. Ever.

To Russia with love

In AD 862, the Finns and Slavs invited the "Rus" (i.e. Viking) Riurikid to come and rule over them, an event which is said by some to mark the beginnings of the Russian Empire.

· 35 ·

Put violence in perspective and take it out of your business

IN THE NINTH CENTURY, the world was still a power vacuum after the Roman empire had collapsed, taking 3,000 years of Mediterranean civilization with it. Europe descended into endless wars, feuds and skirmishes, becoming for centuries a sort of musical chairs of violence – kings and kingdoms could change countless times in a century or even a generation. Compared with this, the level of violence of the Viking attacks was fairly commonplace. The only difference was their clever approach and unlikely level of success.

Even today, cultural, economic and political vacuums bring about violence. Overnight, a storm can turn a city into a lawless nightmare, as in New Orleans. A larger vacuum, for example the situation in Iraq, can bring about violence that is beyond anything the Vikings could ever imagine.

Yet, in the Year of Our Lord 2007, you can find appalling violence that's a daily part of our global economic system. Child labour, pollution and terrible working conditions bring death and suffering to millions every day in the name of sneakers, toys and oil.

It took the Vikings a few centuries to discover that violence is bad business. As Europe began to define itself, the Vikings came to the conclusion that business was actually more profitable than hitting monks over the head. And more fun.

As marketers, we must take the violence out of our businesses, not only for moral reasons, but for the purest economic motives.

Unconvinced? Read on.

· 36 ·

Make a note: slavery is an administrative nightmare

ONE WOULD THINK that the less you pay your employees, the bigger your profit. The cheapest ingredients, the cheapest components, the cheapest production wins. This is why so much manufacturing is done in the third world where wages are low, labour legislation absent and the local dictator conveniently bribed.

Yet, even if we are willing to accept this formula on a moral level, it doesn't add up in dollars and cents for many products. Let's start with a childishly simple example: you make your products using slaves. The only cost is feeding them enough to stay alive and work. What a profit margin! And building escape-proof quarters, of course. But that's it. Oh, yeah, and paying someone to guard them ... and you. (Chances are, you're not the most popular guy on the block ...) And some spies so they don't start plotting. Oh, and somehow you have to get them to do quality work. And you need someone to drag them back when they do escape.

All right then, slavery is not economically feasible. But what about paying nine-year-olds a pittance to work fourteen-hour days? You pick a country where people are starving in the streets, so you don't have any trouble getting workers. You don't have to feed them, house them or even guard them. If they get sick you fire them; if they start organizing you talk to the local police to make the problem go away, preferably in the middle of the night. As for keeping production costs low, there can be no doubt that this is the best solution. However, here is where the problem gets interesting. Labour costs are only a small part of the equation. There are three other factors to be considered: the *brand*, the *technology* and the *target group*.

The strength of a *brand* is a major factor in both price and profit margin. Higher labour costs can easily be offset by other features such as higher quality and social responsibility. In our increasingly transparent global economy it is becoming both easier and more common to question where and how a certain brand is manufactured. Although the average consumer's reactions are still far from a battle cry, there are indications that brands lacking in social responsibility are increasingly at a disadvantage in the marketplace.

Another component is *technology*. Countries with high labour costs are often also highly innovative. When Swatch first started making its plastic watches in Switzerland, a country with some of the highest wages in the world, it had no trouble keeping its product competitively priced. The reason: they had perfected technologies that minimized both assembly time and the number of parts. This, combined with a winning brand concept, gave them a double punch on the market.

And finally, there's the concept of employees as a *target group*. In the early 1900s, Henry Ford kept wages at his factories twice as high as the standard wage to enable his employees to buy the very cars they were making. His revolutionary assembly line had brought manufacturing costs down enough to make this economically feasible, and the symbolic value for the brand was considerable. The employees were hardly a very large group, but the good will and the promotional value were enormous. Every employee with a Ford was a walking billboard for the brand. Newspapers wrote about them, neighbours gossiped, word of mouth flourished. Today, similar effects can be achieved in many markets, by companies big or small.

For example, Light My Fire, the small outdoors company mentioned earlier, does all of its manufacturing in Sweden. At a first glance, it would seem that their plastic Sporks (combined spoon-fork-knife) and meal kits could be made at a fraction of the cost in a cheap labour country. Yet, in this case, the products are made of PP and PC plastic, a high-tech material that requires cutting-edge technology rare in China or India. Light My Fire, in a move that combined social conscience, business acumen and a touch of irony, took over Electrolux's state-of-the-art factory for making plastic vacuum cleaner shells. When the household appliance giant moved that part of its manufacturing to Hungary, they left behind world-class facilities and a gaping hole in the local small-town economy. By re-employing some of the experts from the former Electrolux factory, Light My Fire now has some of the best minds in the business and virtually unlimited capacity. They have also added good will and a powerful new component to the brand.

The story has attracted a fair amount of attention in the media and will continue to do so for a long time to come as the company continues to grow in both sales and profitability.

· 37 ·

Empower your women

We women are free. We only stay with our men as long as it pleases us, and leave them when we no longer like them

– Viking woman to Spanish visitor, AD 850

TO THE SHOCK of many foreign observers of the time, Viking women considered themselves to be equal, a view shared by most Viking men. Women were free to marry and divorce as they chose. Women ran farms and businesses, and they held influential positions in society and were often trusted to take over their husbands' affairs when they went off on trips, often for months or years at a time. Viking women even had the right to inheritance dating back as far as the AD 400s, a right that would take women in the rest of the Europe well over a thousand years more to obtain.

When a couple married, both the bride and groom were expected to bring a dowry of equal value to contribute to the household. If the marriage didn't work out, the husband was expected to return the wife's share of the household. The actual wedding ceremony entailed several days of feasting and drinking and the public consummation of the marriage. The wedding guests followed the couple into their bedroom with torches to see for themselves the betrothed physically consummating the union before the party could go on.

Married men were allowed to have mistresses, but only with the permission of their wives. Failure to get permission could result at best in fines, at worst in a very quick divorce. Other legitimate grounds for divorce were physical abuse, being a bad lover, displaying cowardice or dressing in an unmanly manner.

All of this sounds like just another day in Hollywood, but there is an important point. Over a thousand years before Hollywood or the sexual revolution even existed, Vikings had learned an important lesson. Equality and democracy are essential tools to success in any undertaking. These are more than just pretty words or ideals to aspire to. They actually pay off for everyone concerned.

When social scientists set out to measure the state of different countries around the world, they used to look at GDP, the average standard of living, the level of education and the like. Data processing technology, applications and raw computing power have opened the way for more complex and nuanced comparisons of how countries are doing on the world market. These new indexes often include such factors as sexual equality, equal pay for equal work and level of education of men compared to women.

The Trade Development Index of the United Nations Conference on Trade and Development (UNCTAD) has created a

Trade Development Index (TDI). The index takes into account structural factors such as infrastructure and public administration; trade policies, access to foreign markets and the level of economic, social and gender development. A total of 29 indicators are evaluated: from health and education expenditure per capita to level of corruption and share of GDP per capita of women compared to men. In UNCTAD's report for 2005, Denmark, Sweden and Norway ranked first, fourth and fifth, with the US and the UK second and third on the index.

Other indexes, some that don't even take women into account, often come to similar conclusions. Social inclusion, equality and democracy are just plain good for business. On a national scale or in an organization. It is a fact: there is a direct correlation between women's level of equality and economic success.

Or to put it another way: fifty years ago, Tiger Woods wouldn't even have been let into the clubs where he plays. How many 1950s Tiger Woodses are there in your company or in your organization? How many should there be? What amazing talents are being excluded?

Racism and sexism just don't pay. Any capitalist can see that.

AD 930

*In this year, Norsemen in the colony of Iceland held an
Althing (literally "all thing") at Thingvellir. Laws were
made, judgements passed, disputes settled. This, the world's
first parliament, consisted mostly of men, although a number
of widows and women who ran farms and businesses were
probably also represented.*

*In 2006, 47 per cent of Sweden's parliament consisted of
women.*

· 38 ·

Competition is nonsense

ONE OF THE UGLIER aspects of human nature is the myth of competition – one wins while the others lose. Competition is revered by some cultures and practically worshipped by Americans. The belief is that competition produces better products and creates a better society.

If we look at the facts, this is just not true.

Competition in a society or an organization does not bring out the best in us, nor does it produce better results. Calling competition a false god today is a bit like claiming that the world was round in the middle ages – it's a very obvious observation that goes back thousands of years, but few people want to even consider it, because it seems so threatening to their world view. Even people who have deep reservations about the state of the society and respect the idea of teamwork will find the idea of questioning competition deeply offensive.

In his classic book *No Contest*, Alfie Kohn cites hundreds of clinical, cross-cultural and case studies in education, science and business. The results are overwhelmingly clear – trying to *win over others* and trying to *do well* are two completely different things with very different results. Time and again it has been proven that cooperation produces better results than competition. Children learn better when working together than when competing against each other. Corporations are more efficient when built upon a culture of cooperation and democracy, rather than hierarchy and competition.

In 1981, social psychologists David and Roger Johnson at the University of Minnesota published an analysis of 122 studies of performance in competitive versus cooperative situations. The studies, carried out from 1924 to 1980, showed not only that cooperation promoted better achievement in a majority of the cases, but that the more complicated the task, the greater the advantages of cooperation.

At the University of Texas at about the same time, Robert Helmreich investigated the correlation between achievement and three traits: devotion to work, mastery and competitiveness. First he surveyed 103 male Ph.D. scientists and rated them for achievement by the number of times their work was cited by colleagues. These scientists were asked to fill in questionnaires to ascertain how they rated on the three traits. The results showed that the higher a scientist rated on achievement, the higher he rated on job devotion and mastery, but the *lower* he rated on competitiveness.

The results startled Helmreich, who had expected the exact opposite correlation – that competitiveness spurred achievement. He duplicated the study, this time with academic psychologists. The results were same. Not satisfied, he turned to what he thought would be a hotbed of competition – successful businessmen. This study rated businessmen's relative achievement according to salary and surveyed them on the same three traits: job devotion, mastery and competitiveness. Again, the findings showed that the higher the salary, the higher the job devotion and mastery, but the *lower* the competitive attitude.

Helmreich went on to conduct the same study on female undergraduate students, airline pilots and airline reservation agents. All seven studies showed a *negative correlation* between competitiveness and achievement.

Once you start looking for them, you'll find hundreds of similar studies with similar findings. In education the difference between extrinsic competitive rewards (working for grades, gold stars and student of the month) versus intrinsic rewards (interest and mastery) are especially clear.

Of course, the Vikings knew all this a thousand years ago, without a single study.

· 39 ·

If you want to motivate, forget reward and punishment

WE'VE BEEN TOLD that reward is a much better motivator than punishment for so long that we've missed the point entirely. Reward and punishment are equally ineffectual ways of getting the best out of people – they are just two sides of the same coin.

People take it as an article of faith that people in an organization are motivated by incentives: bonuses, prizes, employee of the month awards, etc. Yet even those who swear by their incentive plans can't get them to work. External rewards just do not work. Rewards increase efficiency only marginally in the short run and decrease it in the long run. When the task being performed involves creativity, reward programmes are the kiss of death. When people in an organization compete for a prize, teamwork suffers and the gap between workers and supervisors grows. People become over-cautious, learn less and take fewer chances. Those who are not rewarded take the lack of reward as a punishment. Those who *are* rewarded worry about not being rewarded in the future.

In his book *Punished by Rewards* Alfie Kohn cites at least seventy studies confirming that rewards tend to undermine interest in the task at hand, making it one of the most thoroughly replicated findings in the field of social psychology. External rewards are not merely ineffectual but actually counterproductive. Those who are offered a reward for doing something (or, in some of the studies, for doing it well) actually do lower quality work than subjects offered no reward at all.

And then, again, there's common sense. Two things make people do things in their lives: external factors and internal factors. External factors include such things as the need to make a living and the need for social acceptance of some sort. Internal factors include the need to be master over your own life, to follow your dreams, to learn, to develop, to be needed, to respect yourself. The most powerful of the two is by far the internal. External motivators such as rewards in a workplace are like snacks for dogs.

The best motivator is a democratic and supportive working environment.

In a study by Families and Work Institute from the early 1990s, a randomly selected sample of 3,400 men and women in the USA ranked "salary/wage" only sixteenth in a list of twenty reasons for taking a job, well behind such factors as open communication, stimulating work, control over work content and the opportunity to gain new skills.

Moving beyond reward and punishment means a return to basic human values. Alfie Kohn offers an elegant formula for motivation, his "three C's of quality":

... Choice, collaboration and content. Choice means workers should participate in making decisions about what they do. Collaboration means they should be able to work together in effective teams. Content refers to the job's tasks. To do a good job, people need a good job to do.

– from *Punished by Rewards*

Spoken like a true Viking. Vikings in the same expedition killed each other over women, too much alcohol, bad drugs and general crankiness, but rarely over money.

Why? They:

1. enjoyed what they were doing (pillaging, etc.);

2. all had a say in what they were doing (pillaging, etc.);

3. all felt they were making a contribution (pillaging, etc.);

and

4. all felt that they were in control of their own destiny (pillaging, etc.).

Replace the word pillaging in the above paragraph with whatever your organization does and you will begin to see the wisdom of the Viking way.

· 40 ·

Talk is cheap, but still overpriced

Talk sense or be silent
– from "Hávamál"

Nobody is completely stupid, if he can be silent
– from "The Saga of Grettir the Strong"

THERE'S AN OLD SWEDISH JOKE about two shoemakers. Year after year they've sat behind their benches working silently and glancing out through the shop window. One day a white horse passes by in the street outside.

"Look, a white horse," says one.

The other nods silently and goes back to work. They work silently together for another month until the same white horse passes again.

"Look, there's that white horse again."
"Enough already about that horse!"

Vikings were great story-tellers, but had little patience with small talk. One of the first historical accounts of the Vikings from AD 789 tells of three Viking ships landing in Portland on the south coast of England. The boats full of bearded visitors caused a sensation and the King ordered Beaduheard, his reeve (chief magistrate), to bring the strangers to his residence in Dorset. Beaduheard, in the grand tradition of civil servants all over the world, was long on words and short on charm. The Vikings – cold, tired, hungry and cranky – lost patience and gave the little man the dubious distinction of being the first recorded fatality of the Viking raids.

"Enough already about that white horse!"

Much of the power of the Viking Manifesto lies in combining great story-telling with a no-nonsense approach to business. Minimize small talk, maximize story-telling. If marketing people spent half as much time creating great stories as they did making small talk in meetings, your average company could cut its marketing budget in half.

Nowadays, Vikings are unarmed, even docile, but they still have great respect for the power of a saga and great impatience with needless small talk.

So how do you distinguish small talk from good stories?

Easy. If you remembered it 24 hours later and told it to someone else it was a story. If you didn't, it was small talk.

· 41 ·

Resurrect the lost art of decision-making

AS A SOCIETY we are moving farther and farther from intuition and common sense. We've traded our world views for niches, our wise men for specialists. We have more information, but fewer frameworks to evaluate it. We must make more decisions, but have less time.

A renaissance of intuition awaits all who are ready for it. Take the step. Let's start with decision-making, for example. All important decisions should be made as follows:

1. Consider all relevant facts.
2. Consider all figures carefully.
3. Read all studies.
4. Put all documents in 1, 2 and 3 above in that wonderful unmarked round folder sometimes referred to as the trash.
5. Look out the window.
6. Listen to your instincts.

Of course you can always skip steps 4–6. In 1978, half a dozen marketing consultants got paid $52,000 for doing just that.

Their advice was historic:

"No one will ever buy Swedish vodka. The bottle doesn't work and the name ... Absolut? Come on!"

· 42 ·

Keep people honest

Be honest and keep your hand on your sword
– anonymous Viking chieftain

THE BEST WAY to avoid being cheated is to be honest. This piece of advice goes beyond karma and "everything that goes around comes around." It's good Viking business. You must be forewarned, forearmed, ready for bloodshed, and honest.

An observation: ever noticed how those who are involved in the most disputes and litigation are often people who are on the slightly shady side of the street? Interestingly it seems that those who are cheated the most are often the cheaters themselves. Dishonesty is one of the major causes of dishonesty.

The key to all relationships is mutual gain. If the terms of an agreement are lopsided or unfair to either side, it will always be broken. Even if a contract is signed in blood, the disadvantaged party will always find a way to get out of it. All business relationships must be fair – both must feel that they have made a good deal and a good deal more. The parties must *need* each other. As an honest man, you must see to it that the person you are doing business with knows what he is doing. If he is ignorant about something that will adversely affect his interests, you must inform him. For moral reasons, yes, but also for practical reasons. When he finds out that you knew that you were getting the better of him he will try to even things up.

Mutual need and mutual gain are great ways of instilling integrity within the organization as well. Creating an atmosphere where everyone is dependent on everyone else brings out the best in people. Even mafiosi can work together with a certain degree of honour when they are in a win–win situation where everyone depends on one another.

And then there is the accountability factor. To get people in your own organization to be honest, you must be even more honest. If you wish them to give you their best, you must give them your best. Looking out for number one means looking out for everyone else. People in an organization put a high value on being treated with respect. Mutual respect is one of the best team-builders.

The sword is the second part of the honesty equation. The sword is knowing your product, your market, the law (here is where you take your lawyers out of their cages). It is also knowing how to launch a surprise attack on those foolish enough not to play fair. Legal solutions are great, but time consuming. Parallel to any frontal legal attack you must strike back full force with other Viking style tactics as well. There are more ways to combat pirating and copyright and trademark infringement, for example, than you can imagine. Let's look at some inspiring examples.

· 43 ·

Plagiarize the plagiarist –
an original idea worth copying

MORE AND MORE of the world's wealth is being tied up in the originality of the brand. As such, the power of the brand is becoming both more attractive and more vulnerable to plagiarism. How does one deal with trademark thieves, hackers, crackers and low-cost factories in Asia?

Ulrika Hydman-Vallien, a Swedish artist known for her popular and very characteristic glass designs, was once the victim of blatant plagiarism. Another less well-known artist had used Ulrika's simplistic hand-painted designs on a line of products as a sort of parody. The degree of parody, however, was zero; this was plagiarism plain and simple. The artist considered the usual channels: lawyers, lawsuits and the like, but decided upon a better attack. She took the line of products with her plagiarized designs and copied them.

She plagiarized the plagiarizer and lifted the line a few notches in quality. This new plagiarism of the plagiarism sold well while the original plagiarism sold badly. What's more, the story got substantial coverage in the media at the time and years later still pops up in other media. A goldmine of sales, PR and media instead of a long, costly and not necessarily profitable legal battle.

By going Viking she swapped legal fees and years of frustration for revenge of the best kind: poetic justice. A successful lawsuit can give you a large settlement and a few paragraphs on page 37. A bit of poetic justice and a good story will buy you coverage and word of mouth for years. (For example in this book.)

In a digital age, both copying and manufacturing take place at a dizzying rate. Anyone who has put sweat, blood and tears into developing a real brand is at risk of losing it overnight. Distributing copycat brands and products to every corner of the globe no longer takes months or years, but can be done in a matter of weeks.

While brand pirating is a real danger, there are things you can do to minimize it. The biggest factor is the most obvious – the character of the brand. The stronger the brand's personality, the stronger its resistance. But what about purely intellectual property such as music and films? Very few people are willing to pay $25 for a store-bought CD or DVD that they can get for free on the web. No amount of branding of the content is going to make any difference.

In the 1990s, when the financial fallout from the web started to show, the record companies and movie studios put their heads together and came up with a futile idea – smoke them out of their caves. They talked tough, went after file-sharing sites and went zero tolerance. Although their actions did produce a lot of soundbites, it didn't sell much music. In fact, sales continued to fall.

They thought like lawyers, not like businessmen.

They had all forgotten their history. When radio came, everyone feared for record sales, but in the long run sales went up. When TV came, the film studios panicked, but again the market for their products ended up growing. Then came the VCR, and again panic, and again increased revenues eventually. In the short run, digital technology is a much larger paradigm shift than anything that has come before it, yet it will probably result in unprecedented new sales. The only way to profit from this shift is to be part of it.

If the entertainment industry had been entrepreneurs instead of accountants, they would have invested early and heavily in their own full-scale download sites with discount tunes and films – a strategy that would have meant short-term profit dips, but long-term gold. As it was, the entertainment industry sat out the beginning of the shift from disc to digital and let Apple pioneer downloading with iTunes. Even with its original meagre offerings, iTunes took off like a rocket – which, if the industry plays its cards right, may actually be a second great opportunity for the industry to make a go of it digitally.

In ten to twenty years, most music and film will be downloaded. The jury is still out on what form it will take and how the revenues will be generated, but they will make and break giants.

Time to get on board.

• 44 •

Put lawyers in the last boat

There's a rule of thumb for written contracts. The same deal will require a one page contract in Sweden, four pages in England or sixteen pages in the USA. And guess where you're most likely to go to court ...

– anonymous multinational executive

LAWYERS ARE AT BEST a necessary evil and at worst a positive handicap. In the boardroom, in marketing strategy, in creative decisions – lawyers in the USA are often on the front lines of business. The rest of the world finds this a bit odd. Considering the climate of fear created by the nature of America's litigious society, the position of the American lawyer is understandable, yet counter-productive.

Vikings thought of their cargo in terms of livestock and deadstock. Livestock was cows for food, oxen to pull the ships across land and other things that were productive. Deadstock consisted of those things that were necessary, but unproductive. They were put in the last boat. Lawyers are deadstock.

They are a necessary evil to protect you from unnecessary evil.

A lawyer goes through years and years of training in the art of paranoia and saying "it can't be done." Giving lawyers too much of a say is a guarantee that an organization will stagnate and die. Lawyers should be brought in late in the decision-making process and consulted on specific issues – legal issues. Lawyers should be kept out of the boardroom, away from marketing meetings and the other side of town from anything creative.

Lawyers are smart; good lawyers, brilliant. Yet many have a fatal weakness that can bring down an organization as quickly as any class action suit – a lack of intuition. Lawyers are great to have on board. They are by far the most valuable cargo.

On the last boat.

Mead

A strong alcoholic beverage made from fermenting water, honey and yeast and flavoured with malt, hops, berries, fruits or spices. Vikings drank it for festive occasions, while they drank a low-alcohol beer as a mealtime beverage. If given a choice, however, they preferred wine, a much valued item from the trade routes on the continent.

· 45 ·

Use creative accounting
for a better world

Money wisely given always comes back to the giver
– old proverb

IN AN ARTICLE about the California environmental movement in the 1990s, one of the authors (Steve Strid) wrote:
"One of the most exciting trends in environmentalism today
may just be ... accounting."

This may well turn out to be more than just a catchy introduction; accountants may well turn out to be the environmental
heroes of the future.

In the same article a well-known environmental activist said
that nothing concrete ever happened in environmentalism
until there's a buck to be made. Protests rarely provide practical solutions to socio-economic-environmental problems.
Sadly enough, things don't begin happening until the capitalist machinery senses a profit in cleaning up.

To date, most corporations' environmental measures have

been an effort to court the growing group of consumers who take environmental issues seriously. This phenomenon has led to some real changes, along with mountains of green-wash media campaigns with big-eyed fuzzy bear cubs.

As the global village shrinks and corporate globalization grows, waste and destruction will gradually creep closer and closer to the balance sheet. As cause and effect gradually move closer to the centres of profit, there will be a realization that pollution is a concrete expense. In the old days, corporations could freely dump whatever they needed, wherever they needed. Then, as the connection was made between pollutants and cancer, CO_2 and the greenhouse effect, wasteful consumption and world poverty, accountants began seeing that pollution was costing corporations money in ways they had never realized.

If cancer rates go up 20 per cent at and near a certain factory, that company stands to lose money on decreased efficiency (employees concerned about getting sick or concerned about loved ones getting sick), increased turnover (people actually getting sick or dying), increased litigation costs, increased lobbying (and bribery) costs, and, probably most expensive, increased media costs for the environmentally concerned ad campaigns. A good accountant will enter all these sorts of expenditures into the books.

Meaningful and sincere contributions to the community, to education, to day-care and healthcare not only bring good will, but also reduced costs in almost every area of a company's business. Crime and domestic misery go down, resulting in reduced costs of doing business, while the resulting decrease in poverty means increased buying power.

For those that don't see an obvious economic profit from giving to the community, there is a dollars and cents example.

After World War II, the US aid programme the Marshall Plan poured $13 billion into rebuilding Europe to restore industrial and agricultural production, create financial stability and stimulate trade.

The war had been bad news in many ways. One of the USA's most profitable export markets had been ravaged by all manner of destruction and, almost as bad in crass economic terms, America had a surplus of dollars, a foreign exchange nightmare.

Most of the funds to Europe were in the form of direct grants with the remainder in loans. In the four years of this programme, European countries' GNP grew by 15–25 per cent; Europe quickly prospered and became a key trading partner, resulting in unprecedented profits both for American businesses and American government. The return on investment on every million has probably profited US businesses and government more in the long run than anything they've ever done.

'Tis better to give than receive. And often more profitable.

· 46 ·

Controversy is great, if you're right

IF THERE'S ONE THING that businessmen avoid like the plague, it's controversy. Unfortunately, when you spend too much time playing it safe, the result is often a lacklustre brand.

A bit of controversy is worth its weight in gold. A bit of controversy should be the holy grail of any corporation that wants to get its message out.

Make a stand. Do the right thing.

· 47 ·

Rethink money

ONE OF THE BEST WAYS of succeeding is to take the focus off money. It's a bit like diving for coins at the bottom of a pool – the more you stretch when you approach the bottom, the faster you float up.

Ingvar Kamprad, one of the richest men in the world, doesn't ring a bell with anyone outside Sweden. He is the founder and owner of IKEA. He opened the first IKEA store in the remote Swedish forest town of Älmhult in 1953 as a showroom for his mail-order business, to allow customers to see and touch the products before ordering them. People came from all over the country to Älmhult, and IKEA quickly became more than a popular store – it became a phenomenon.

When the Stockholm IKEA opened in 1965, the opening reception was closer to a rock concert than a store opening, with $10 million in first-year sales. (Today this store alone has gross sales of $120 million.) By the 1970s, the IKEA concept had more or less taken form – clever design, relatively high quality, amazingly low prices, loads of attitude and a Swedish sense of humour. (All the furniture has more or less appropriate Swedish names – a source of smiles for the Swedes, bemused confusion for everyone else.) IKEA was ready to become an international phenomenon.

When IKEA went abroad it kept its name, its Swedish product names, its big stores in low-rent suburbs, its personality. All through its expansion, it even retained much of its small company origins. Founder Kamprad refused to borrow money: IKEA had always been and always would be self-financing. (To his chagrin, he was forced to take out a personal loan for $700,000 when he moved out of Sweden, due to the Swedish currency restrictions in effect at the time. The loan was paid back promptly with a promise *never again*, a promise which he kept.)

In the late 1980s, Ingvar Kamprad was under great pressure to go public; his accountants, his advisers and even his own board were for the idea, but he refused. He wanted IKEA to grow at the speed warranted by the market, not by the shareholders. IKEA should have the option of growing more slowly or not growing at all, if it was the right thing to do. Through sheer stubbornness, and the right of ownership, he held fast. The rest of the company gradually came around when it became clear that IKEA was continuing to grow brilliantly under its own steam.

Today, with sales of $22.5 billion, 237 stores and half a billion visitors a year, IKEA's economy is quickly approaching that of a small country.

The author of a recent book about IKEA was extremely surprised to find that not one of the dozen or so people who have been with the company from the start ever mentioned money as a motivator. Not in the beginning and not now. Salaries are and always have been low at the company, especially at the management level. Ingvar Kamprad is famous for using public transport, buying his own appliances at the local discount outlet and using the same comfy chair for 32 years – a 1974 IKEA Poäng. When he once stayed at a hotel in New York he was upgraded to the penthouse when, unbeknownst to him, someone realized that he owned the hotel. Kamprad immediately asked to be downgraded again.

The point is that some of the most innovative ideas about money are thousands of years old. Work hard, make more than you spend, don't buy things you can't afford, reinvest, produce quality, have something to say, help make the world a little better.

Oh God, protect me from the wrath of the Norsemen!

– ninth-century English prayer

Oh God, where the hell is that Allen wrench!

– 21st-century IKEA customer

· 48 ·

Two approaches to dealing with crisis – proactive or poodle

WHEN DISASTER STRIKES, when the media starts foaming at the digital mouth, there are two approaches – proactive or poodle.

Proactive means that you take the lead and fight back – either head on head or with communications judo.

Monte Reid, film trailer narrator, actor, copywriter and cowboy, tells a wonderful story:

> There was once a Texas company making chili con carne that had the biggest disaster possible – a consumer had found a rat in one of their cans. Panic ensued, but the shrewd cowboy factory owner simply smiled and said, "Buy me sixty seconds of TV time for tomorrow night, son."

> The quality control people in the factory did their jobs, the batch was traced, video from the factory cameras were examined. When it was time to send off a video to the local channel for broadcast, even the production manager felt a bit calmer.

"Hi. I'm Jack Howling, the owner of Pepe's Chili," the commercial began. "Two days ago, a Doug Smith of Fort Worth, Texas, found a rat in a can of our chili. We have checked every last detail of our production facilities and gone through everything in our factory to find the cause of this horrible accident. A check of our video records shows that one of our employees, a disgruntled distant relative, was responsible for putting the rat in that can, hoping to ruin the family business. If you stop buying our products, I understand. But, I would like to make it up to you. Here's what I suggest. We will put a plastic mouse in one of the next million cans of chili. The first person that buys a can with the mouse inside will be awarded one million dollars in cash by me personally, as a symbol of our never-ending quest to make the best product possible. Until then, once again, accept my deepest apologies. Thank you."

Sales of Pepe's Chili soared, PR and good will flowed and the company prospered.

In the case of the rat, the strong and emotional response was countered by an equally strong and emotional response, far beyond what anyone had expected.

In other situations it is advisable to take a completely different approach: the poodle.

"Doing a full poodle" is a Scandinavian expression coined by Norwegian Pål Jebsen, CEO of the Swedish branch of Burson-Marsteller. In reference to a Swedish scandal a few years back, Jebsen said, "The best thing he can do is a *hel pudel* [literally, a full poodle]."

"A full poodle?"

"Yeah, my wife has a poodle, and when she raises her voice, the dog rolls over on its back with its paws in the air. It does a *full poodle*."

(The expression has since crossed the North Sea and has been taken up by the *Financial Times* in a number of articles as "doing a whole poodle." *Hel* in Swedish means both "whole" and "full", and in this phrase the authors prefer "full", as in full-Nelson as opposed to half-Nelson, and full-blown as opposed to half-assed.)

When actor Hugh Grant, for example, was caught with his pants down with a Hollywood prostitute, he went on talk-shows non-stop for months and did a full poodle. He lay down on his proverbial back, raised his paws and said, "Sorry, sorry, sorry ... what was I thinking ... ." Even his grandmother got in on the act: "I tell my friends that he'd had a few too many drinks with the boys and did something a bit naughty."

If you have no defence, do a full poodle. And if you can get your grandmother in on it, all the better.

⋆ 49 ⋆

Take marketing studies
with a pinch of salt

IF YOU HAD ASKED one million consumers in 1978 if they needed a computer at home, practically no one would have answered yes. Four years later Apple became the first computer company with sales of more than $1 billion ...

The general rule of thumb for Scandinavian companies is that they spend far less on formal market research than their counterparts in other countries. Part of this has to do with simple economics – their media budgets are smaller. As their market is much smaller, their media less expensive and their populations tiny, it is often less expensive to spend budgets on trying things out "live" on the market directly than going through a long-drawn-out study period. Many Scandinavian multinationals consider their home markets more as "test markets" than as major sources of revenue. (Many of these companies even have English as the official internal language for all documentation and communication.) The result is that many innovative concepts that would have been studied to death actually make it out to the market where they can prove their worth.

At IKEA in the USA, Swedish management noticed that their drinking glasses were not selling well, while crystal vases were selling so fast they could barely keep them in stock. It very quickly became clear that Americans found the European glasses far too small and that the IKEA vases were perfect for that Super-Size-with-lots-of-ice experience.

IKEA does surprisingly little market research for such a large company, which leaves them open to these sorts of miscalculations. Yet this same shoot-from-the-hip attitude is one reason that they have been so far ahead of their time so many times. They've always dared to trust their instincts and dared to make mistakes.

Market studies giveth and market studies taketh away. Security, yes, but at the expense of innovation. Listening too much to what others say can drown out your own inner voice. Very few of the great innovations of our times – probably none of them – were the result of any sort of formal studies.

The right finger raised in the air at the right time can be more than enough to change an industry. Or the world.

∙ 50 ∙

Don't leave luck to chance

AT THE END of the day (and the end of this book), luck is probably the biggest factor in everything we do. Something that important is far too important to sit around and wait for.

The harder you work, the more times you fail, the more variations you try, the luckier you'll get.

When someone tells you that you have a one-in-a-million chance of succeeding, just smile. The chances of you ever having been born are trillions to one.

A million to one looks pretty good to us.

The generous and bold have the best lives,
Are seldom beset by cares,
But the base man sees bogies everywhere
And the miser pines for presents

– from "Hávamál"

THE END

Appendix: The latest thing from AD 900

(the Vikings live on...)

The Lord of the Rings – Much of the material and language of Tolkien's books was inspired by Norse mythology. The success of the recent films is a testament to the timelessness of the pagan invader.

Toys – LEGO, Playmobil and other toymakers all over the world continue to introduce new Viking themes.

Cities – The Vikings founded Kiev, Novgorod, Dublin, York and half a dozen other cities that are still around. (They also burned down about a hundred more that are also still around ...)

Russia – Claims that the Vikings established the beginnings of the Russian empire are disputed, but the word "Russian" probably does come from *rus* – as Swedish traders were referred to in eastern Europe and Russia.

A fair part of the English language – Although Old Norse and Old English came from common roots, there are some 900 words the Vikings made a part of everyday language in England. Nautical words such as *starboard, keel* and *rig*; earthy, soulful words such as *die, dregs, mire, slaughter* and *rugged*; and some words that we could hardly get along without such as *they, their, them, law, take, get, ugly, angry* and *freckle*. And let's not forget the famous *sk-* series: *skid, skin, skull, skulk* and *sky*.

Geography – There are hundreds of place names with the ending *-by*, which means "town" or "farm", such as Whitby, Derby, Rugby, Thoresby; *-thorpe*, meaning "village", as in Althorp and Linthorpe; and *-toft*, meaning "homestead", as in Langtoft and Eastoft.

Bibliography

A. C. Baugh, *A History of the English Language*, 5th edition.
Routledge, London, 2002

Frans G. Bengtsson, *Röde orm*, originally published in Swedish in
1941–5, Norstedts, Stockholm.
English translation, *The Long Ships*, HarperCollins; new
impression, 1984. Translated by Michael Meyer.
(Note: quotations appearing in this book are new translations
from the original Swedish by Steve Strid.)

Ian Black (European editor), "Flat-pack denial as IKEA boss
named richest in world", *Guardian*, 6 April 2004

Oliver Burkeman, "The Miracle of Älmhult" (Parts 1 & 2),
Guardian, 17 June 2004

David Crystal, *The Cambridge Encyclopaedia of the English Language*,
Cambridge University Press, Cambridge, 2003

("Doing a full poodle" discussion): "OBSERVER: Dog days",
Financial Times.com, 21 February 2003

Richard Donkin, "Survey – Classified Recruitment: Less is more for the future of work ...", *Financial Times*, 19 April 2001 (web)

Encyclopaedia Britannica (deluxe edition CD), 2005

Luke Harding, "1974 IKEA chair, one careful owner, not for sale", *Guardian*, 20 December 2006

"Hávamál" (literally: "The Sayings of the High One") One of the poems of the *Poetic Edda*, a collection of mythological and heroic poems of unknown authorship dating from AD 800 to 1100. The manuscript was probably compiled in the later thirteenth century. We've used the translation by W. H. Auden & P. B. Taylor. This text is available in a number of different editions and collections. One example is *Norse Poems*, Faber & Faber, London, 1983. Another is *Hávámal: Words of the High One*, Kessinger Publishing, Montana, 2004

Catharina Ingelman-Sundberg, *Boken om Vikingarna* ("The Book of the Vikings"), Bokförlaget Prisma, Stockholm, 2000

Catharina Ingelman-Sundberg, *Forntida kvinnor* ("Ancient Women"), Bokförlaget Prisma, Stockholm, 2004

Bodil Jönsson, *Tio tankar om tid* ("Ten Thoughts About Time"), Brombergs Bokförlag, Stockholm, 1999

Jukkasjärvi Ice Hotel website: www.icehotel.com

Alfie Kohn, *No Contest: The Case Against Competition*, Houghton Mifflin Company, New York, 1986, revised edition 1992

Alfie Kohn, *Punished By Rewards: The Trouble with Gold Stars, Incentive Plans, A's, Praise, and Other Bribes*, Mariner Books (Houghton Mifflin Company), New York, 1999

The Kon-Tiki Museum, Bygdøy, Norway: www.kon-tiki.no

Lego corporate site: www.lego.com/eng/info/

Light My Fire corporate site: www.light-my-fire.com

James G. Lowe, senior editor, Merriam-Webster Inc., "Scandinavian Influence on English", from Scripps National Spelling Bee: www.spellingbee.com/cc07/Week14/scand.shtml

Anne-Charlotte Malm and Roger Garman, "Så kan Sverige möta morgondagens köpkraft" ("How Sweden should meet tomorrow's buying power"), *Dagens Industri*, 13 December 2006

Metro International corporate site: www.metro.lu

"The National Study of the Changing Workforce," conducted by the Families and Work Institute. Described in the *New York Times*, 19 September 1993, p. F21

Newspaper trade organizations:

World Association of Newspapers (online)
www.wan-press.org/

Editor and Publisher Yearbook (online)
Gives circulation figures for newspapers in Canada and USA
www.editorandpublisher.com/

Audit Bureau of Circulations
www.accessabc.com

Nobel Prize site: www.nobelprize.org

Will Pavia, "The Vikings are coming", *The Times*, 27 November 2006

Sam Roberts, "Fatter, Taller and Thirstier Americans", *New York Times*, 15 December 2006, Section A, Page 27

Peter Sawyer (editor), *Oxford Illustrated History of the Vikings*, Oxford University Press, 1999

Steve Strid and Kevin Billinghurst, "From the Margins to the Mainstream", *Tomorrow* magazine, Spring 1990

Strix Television: www.strix.se

Sveriges Television ("Sweden's Television"): svt.se

On Sweden's Parliament website: *"Kvinnor i riksdagen"* ("Women in Parliament"), 21 November 2006: www.riksdagen.se

Henry David Thoreau, *Walden; Or, Life in the Woods*, originally published 1854

Bertil Torekull, *Historien om IKEA, Ingvar Kamprad berättar*, ("The Story of IKEA as Told by Ingvar Kamprad"), Wahlström & Widstrand, Stockholm, 1998

Trade and development Index, 2005, United Nations Conference on Trade and Development (UNCTAD); United Nations, New York and Geneva, 2005

US Census Report, 2007, (www.census.gov)

Denise Winterman, "The Vikings are coming", BBC News Magazine, 23 November 2006

World Exports 1994-04, World Trade Organization, (www.wto.org)

About the authors

Steve Strid is an American brand consultant who has been behind the scenes in building brands such as Absolut, Magic, Light My Fire, Libresse and Baby Björn. He has worked with multinational corporations and advertising agencies on everything from individual global campaigns to complete strategy and branding programmes. He has also written a play and numerous articles for publications such as the *Sunday Times*, the *Guardian*, the *Los Angeles Times*, *Innova* and *Reflexions*.

As the North American area director for The Absolut Company (1989–95) and Director of the Absolut Akademi (1996–2001), **Claes Andréasson** had the good fortune to have been part of a legendary marketing story. Claes is a full-blooded Swede with respect for history, traditions and crayfish.

Their work together has resulted in some bizarre adventures in marketing, management and education, but also some record sales and insights into exciting new trends.

The Viking Manifesto has been translated into eleven languages. Please visit ***www.vikingmanifesto.com*** for more details.

Illustration credits

Page 7: A 7th-century stone carving from the Swedish island of Gotland. Drawing by Adam A.

Page 159: The god Thor with his hammer. From an 11th-century bronze statuette, probably a gaming piece, found in northern Iceland. Drawing by Anna Hernaeus.

Also published by Marshall Cavendish

GREAT IKEA!
A BRAND FOR ALL THE PEOPLE
Elen Lewis

*"There has been a revolution in taste in recent years that Ikea
has championed like no other – bringing well-designed products,
at accessible prices, to an entirely new customer base. This is a
comprehensive and enjoyable read about a brand that has not only
changed the way we shop, but also the way we think about modern
design."* **Suzanne Imre, editor,** *Livingetc*

Elen Lewis gives a witty and informative account of the ideas,
principles, and history behind Ikea – a brand as well as a
philosophy that has changed the way we furnish our homes,
and made Swedish meatballs an essential part of the shopping
experience. She explains how Ikea arose from the vision of one
man, Ingvar Kamprad, and how his belief – that you change
customer expectations rather than the product itself – has
created a worldwide icon.

Ikea has made stylish furniture affordable to everyone; but is
it to our advantage that we now regard it as a disposable item?
Where did those strange furnishing names come from? How
come Ikea executives never stay at the Marriott? Why didn't
Ikea furniture go down well at first in the United States? And is
there really a secret route through the store for those who want
to skip the kitchen and bathroom displays?

This is a book for brand professionals and consumers alike. Take
it with you when you next purchase a Billy bookcase.

ISBN 978–1-905736–16–4/£8.99 Paperback

Also published by Marshall Cavendish

ONE

A CONSUMER REVOLUTION FOR BUSINESS

Stefan Engeseth

"Some people believe you need to think outside of the box. That's silly. What you need is a much bigger box. Stefan Engeseth will help you find one." **Seth Godin, marketing guru and author of** *Purple Cow*

The power of the consumer is greater than it has ever been. Yet the gap between what companies promise and what consumers experience has never been wider. If companies are to survive and thrive in this age of the consumer, they need to interact with their customers. They need to let customers into their processes for creating new products and services, and even into their marketing and selling.

Most big companies still run their business as a monologue. Though they may try to talk to customers on a one-to-one basis, they aren't really listening. But in a time of ad-skipping, blogs, hate websites and consumer activism, they can't afford to stay so aloof. Brands are powerful only when they are relevant to consumers – when companies take what's important to the target audience and make it an integral part of the brand. For that to happen, brand and consumers must work together as one.

Drawing on a wealth of anecdotes, examples and cutting-edge ideas, this revolutionary new book offers methods, tools and inspiration to bring customers closer to your company. *ONE* is nothing less than a new marketing manifesto. Read it and learn how to make consumer power work for your company, not against it.

ISBN 978–0-462–09941–5/£9.99 Paperback